James Ellis was born in east Belfast in 1931. Son of a sheet-metal worker, he was educated on scholarships at Methodist College and Queen's University Belfast, where he read English, French and Philosophy. A Tyrone Guthrie scholarship took him to the Bristol Old Vic Theatre School. During the 1950s he worked mainly as a theatre director. His most notable production was Sam Thompson's controversial 'Over the Bridge', which was later taken on tour in Britain by Laurence Olivier's company. Best known for his work in television and film—mediums in which he has maintained a high-profile for nearly four decades—he has also starred in West End stage productions. As a stage actor he has done seasons at the Barbican with the Royal Shakespeare Company, with the National Theatre and Sir Peter Hall's company at the Old Vic. An accomplished reciter of verse, he has recently recorded for video a version of Belfast poet Paul Yates' long poem, *East*.

DOMESTIC FLIGHT

DOMESTIC FLIGHT

JAMES ELLIS

LAGAN PRESS
BELFAST
1998

Published by
Lagan Press
PO Box 110 BT12 4AB, Belfast

ISBN: 1 873687 30 3 pbk/1 873687 40 0 hbk
Author: Ellis, James
Title: Domestic Flight
1998

Cover Design: Kevin Cushnahan
Set in Palatino
Printed by Noel Murphy Printing, Belfast

for my wife,
Robina

'How passionately and irretrievably,
In what fond flight, how many ways and days!'
—Dante Gabriel Rossetti, 'Souls Beauty'

CONTENTS

Introduction

It began with a sonnet. A famous and colourful wartime headmaster of the Methodist College, Belfast, John Falconer, M.A. (Edin.) known to the poet Robert Greacan and several generations of school boys and girls, including myself, as 'Johnny the Hawk' was initiating us into the primary mysteries of the 'Little Song':

> With this key
> Shakespeare unlocked his heart; the melody
> Of this small lute gave ease to Petrarch's wound ...

Dwelling on the intricacies of its infrastructure—the Spartan disciplines of double-rhymed octave, turn, and sestet, the Shakespearean, Spenserean, and Miltonic variants, and, above all, the shining virtue of its implacable and unalterable brevity his clipped Knoxian delivery suggested at times not so much poetic imagery, as certain Caledonian instruments of torture—the thumbscrew, or the 'Boots'. At the conclusion of this induction I was foolish enough to ask what contribution I might make to the school magazine. The sardonic response was: "Write a sonnet, Ellis." The incident may account for the preponderence of 'fourteen-liners' in this collection.

The verses offered here have accumulated over the last thirty-five or so years, undergoing re-writes and revisions, acceptance and rejection, as and when the spirit has moved me. The most intense activity, however, has taken place over this last decade, accompanied by a sustained effort to translate a body of sixteenth century French verse into persuasive and plausible English.

As a respite from this, I undertook a transcription of the Jason and Medea story to be performed by myself at the Belfast Festival in November, 1992. Using an excellent French prose version as my principal source, I focused on the central core of the Argonautica of Apollonius of Rhodes (Books II and III), rendering it into ten-line blank-verse stanzas. The founder of Lagan Press who attended the festival performance, has, since then, repeatedly asked me for material with a view to publication.

Meanwhile I had been exchanging themes, ideas, and images with a much younger poet, Paul Yates, who remembers me from his childhood as someone 'vaguely famous'. He was raised less than two hundred yards away from the house where my formative youth was spent, but by the time he was growing up I had moved across the Irish Sea, and he recalls me only as a bird of passage, accompanied on one memorable occasion by an exotic female of the species:

Long legs, long hair
In Sinclair's shop, and the lad is only eleven—
The child is taking names, I tell you!

Strangely enough, not much has changed in this area of East Belfast; losses there are, but even of these, traces yet remain— the billiard hall is just a shell, and Bailey's bacon slicer is silenced forever, though a shop is still there, and a sanitised Connswater still flows sluggishly past the pumping station—as Paul succinctly puts it: "We grew up a stone's throw, and a mere thirty years apart."

'Domestic Flight' as an overall title may be construed both literally and metaphorically. In the former sense it relates to a fairly regular to-ing and fro-ing across the Irish Sea, though a decision to make London the home base was made as early as 1960. The first migration, however, took place in 1938, when my father found employment in Cammel Laird's shipyard on Merseyside, though the family was back in Belfast by the outbreak of war in September of the following year. The next significant crossing was in the autumn of 1951, to spend a year at the Bristol Old Vic, with the 'definitive' parting coming almost a decade later; though I have long since lost count of the number of return journeys I have made, by both sea and air. The figurative meaning might imply a breaking away from domesticity, a desire to be rid of provincial restraints in a society where everyone knows everyone else, and everyone else's business; and where puritanical considerations can clip the boldest wings. For all that, the qualifying adjective suggests no impulsive dash to the ends of the earth, but rather a desire to cling on to roots that are precious, and landscapes that are dear—a prodigal who returns not just once, but again, and again, and again!

I hope that travel, as it is meant to, has broadened my mind somewhat, and that with Goldsmith I value my citizenship of the world as I do that of my native place. Recent visits to Eastern Europe and Southern Africa have opened my eyes, my heart, and my mind to new friends, new vistas, and new horizons; and these I have tried to reflect in my latest endeavours:

> Yet all experience is an arch where through
> Gleams that untravell'd world whose margin fades
> Forever and forever when I move.

The vexed question of publication came to a head last year when I was invited to make a contribution to the John Hewitt International Summer School, a prestigious annual gathering of literary men and women which honours the memory of a fine Ulster-born poet. Pressed for a provisional caption to serve as a programme heading and advance publicity title, I chose the vaguely ambiguous 'An Actor's Verses', thinking to compile a garland of purple patches from poets interspersed with personal comments, and my reasons for choosing them. Come the day, no such anthology had been compiled, so I launched recklessly into readings from my own manuscripts, gamely assisted by Miss Margaret D'Arcy, who brought a touch of elegance and class to a handful of translations. The recital was generously received—perhaps actors have a slight advantage in the arena of public reading—but the immediate aftermath was, to me, entirely unforeseen: "Where was the book?", "What about the signed copies?". Only then did I realise that I had walked naked into the market place—a poor pedlar who, after making his pitch, had no wares to peddle! The die was cast.

A pleasant lunch ensued with Margaret, and the two distinguished novelists, Aidan Higgins and Maurice Leitch, at the Londonderry Arms in Carnlough. The former was kind enough to compliment me on a Ronsard translation, the latter was more vehement. In his inimitable and forthright fashion, my old friend Maurice pinned me to the wall: "Until you get between those covers, Jimmy, you are an invisible man; publish and be damned to hell along with the rest of us."

When the exiled Romanian philosopher E.M. Cioran remarked that the publication of a book involved problems similar to those of a wedding or a funeral, I am sure he envisaged wider implications than the formalities and the etiquette, but tor my part I have found that forewords, dedications, acknowledgements, and notes, have added up to one severe and prolonged headache, akin to that of a bride's parent as the day of reckoning draws nigh. Suffice to say, that anyone whose name appears in these words of gratitude will have been in my thoughts at some the preparation of this book, and appreciative or encouraging friends whose names have been omitted will, I hope, forgive me; they are not oversights, but quite simply, examples of mental frailty. Dedications have been decimated at the discretion of the publishers because, as was gently but firmly pointed out, they had become downright silly.

Early exchanges of artistic and literary ideas centred on a little coterie of lively spirits that met in and around Mount Charles, or in the cloistered snugs of the Elbow Room or Crown bars. The group included the painters Basil Blackshaw and T.P. Flanagan—a precocious poetic talent—graphic wizard

Desmond Kinney, the architects Henry Lynch Robinson and Robert McKinstry, and the great all-round and satirist of the great, the good, and the humble, Rowel Friers, whose recent and sudden death is such a loss to us all. John Hewitt—even then an avuncular father figure—often joined the company, as did actors James Greene, Denys Hawthorne, Billy Miller, and Colin Blakeley; and playwrights Sam Thompson, Sam Hanna Bell, John Boyd, and John D. Stewart. Joseph Tomelty, a prolific dramatist and novelist as well as an actor, was, by the early 50s, well on the way to silver screen celebrity, as was Billy Miller, soon to become the film star, Stephen Boyd. The inimitable J.G. Devlin was still the pack leader and mentor of the young actors, though he, too, would soon cross the 'sheugh' to grace the small screen and the London stage with his rare persona and talent as did his protege, the wonderful Colin Blakeley. Harold Goldblatt, who had held the fort for so long as director of the Group Theatre, also departed to enjoy a distinguished late flowering on the English stage and in films. Then, after my short though tempestuous reign as his successor, the sequel that involved the triumphant staging of *Over the Bridge* at the old Empire Theatre, and the subsequent shameful close and demolition of that lovely house of entertainment, I too left the scene. The whimsical and resilient 'Hibbie' Wilmot remained at the Arts Theatre presenting commercial comedy for mass consumption where he had previously offered European and transatlantic plays of consequence, and the resourceful and single-mind Mary O'Malley emerged from her drawing room in Derryvolgie Avenue to found the Lyric Theatre which has become the true inheritor of the 'Group' legacy. Though unable to sustain a permanent company on the scale of the old institution, players of the calibre of John Hewitt, Mark Mulholland and the late Louis Rolston; Stella McCusker, Roma Tomelty, Sheila McGibbon and many others, would have been leading lights in any generation and would likely as not have graced Sir Tyrone Guthrie's Festival of Britain Company had they been around at the time! It is all that mental and artistic interaction of the fifties that I was greatly to miss when I moved to England.

In England, and particularly in its metropolis, the 'Arts' tend to be segregated, specialised, and competitive to a degree, unlike the multicultural communities of other European capitals. There are exceptions to this of course and here and there or from time to time, painters, poets, musicians, actors, dancers, and other performers will drift together in a mutual awareness; but such groups are as ephemeral as a touring play or an ever changing repertory company. By contrast, friendships formed in the fifties in Belfast and Dublin with creative people in every field are as warm and steadfast as ever.

Of course I have made friends over here as well as remaining in touch with colleagues such as Kenneth Branagh, Adrian Dunbar, James Nesbitt, Frances Tomelty, and many others. Old colleagues from a famous television series such as Frank Windsor and Joe Brady are still in touch; we all shared that glow of pride when Colin Welland turned screenwriter and won an Oscar, as when the intrepid Brian Blessed tackled Everest .Graham Reid now lives permanently in London. He and his talented wife Gwen Taylor are never far away from a get-together or a telephone chat, the exchange of ideas a prime consideration. Chiswick neighbours who kept my mind alert included the late Alun Owen, prolific playwright and screenwriter to the Beatles, whose lively observation and keen wit I sadly miss. Adam Adamou, greengrocer extraordinaire and fine photographer was, like myself, another member of that circle. A man who prefers philosophy to small talk, it was he who drew my attention to Cioran's comments on publishing as well as many deeper aspects of his works. Another old friend is the Liverpool playwright and short story writer, Vincent McInerney, a man of many parts and life-enhancing spirit with whom I exchange manuscripts, scenarios and fresh thoughts and ideas, either at his place or mine, together with many a rousing sea shanty or burst of improvisation on the piano.

During a year long sojourn on the Isle of Wight I enjoyed the stimulating company of near neighbours Roger and Diana Sawyer; Roger had written a book on Casement and was preparing another on women of Ireland; I acted as a sort of guide round some Irish ancestral homes from Down to Wexford while he completed his research into family archives, and in return he encouraged my own aspirations to put pen to paper.

I suppose it is true to say that in general the theatre offers a clearer artistic focus than either television or films, for me at any rate. Spells at the Royal Shakespeare Company, the National Theatre, and Sir Peter Hall's Old Vic Company have, over the years, renewed to a certain extent the cutting edge I felt most keenly in my time in the Ulster theatre. Large institutions, however, can also 'dull the edge of husbandry', but I believe that Sir Peter Hall's warm, big-brotherly, and hands on administration in all three play factories avoided depersonalisation to a remarkable extent. The director, however, with whom I have worked most over the years—in theatre, film, television, and sound radio—has been Bill Bryden. He is an unfailing inspiration, and a natural leader who, whether working with star performers or a company collective, can turn a production into an exciting cohesive whole involving personal commitment and interaction among players, designers, musicians, choreographers, and indeed everyone concerned, including of course the writer if he is alive. I have good reason to be grateful for his advice and encouragement and his generosity of spirit in times of crisis.

In Northern Ireland, director, folklorist, and musician Tony McAuley was among the first to cast a critical eye over my attempts at creative writing, and latterly, the poets C.L. Dallat and Anne-Marie Fyfe spoke and wrote words of encouragement. Maggie Stansfield published the translation of a Ronsard sonnet in the magazine Omnibus and Sir Harry Secombe included one of my lyrics in his 'Highway' anthology after I read it on his programme from Bangor, County Down. John Anderson included two of my efforts in the Ulster television

[19]

film "A Bunch of Thyme" and I know that Gerry Kelly has allowed me to recite on his programme more than once, though whether they were ever my own lines I cannot recall. BBC producers who recorded verse translations were Judith Elliot and Pam Brighton, who also directed *Jason and Medea*. Rowel Friers, who designed that event, was then toiling over his superb autobiography, *Drawn from Life*, and reading over the proofs with him spurred me on to renewed metrical efforts. I have many happy memories of that lively household where I was so often a welcome guest, and where his family and his wife, Yvonne, made me feel perfectly at home. Robin Walsh at that time Controller of BBC Northern Ireland, is a valued friend who quietly opens doors and points the way in times of stress.

During the book's actual preparation the visit to southern Africa opened new horizons and threw up fresh imagery and unfamiliar landscapes; these I have tried to reflect in the half dozen pieces which begin with 'Long Haul'. Fellow actor, David Horovitch was also, I discovered, putting pen to paper and it was for both of us an energising experience to exchange images and impressions. He and I, together with Suzanne Harker and Jonathan Firth, took the road to Glenlivet and Great Zimbabwe together, and some of our wide-eyed wonderment is, I hope, reflected in the poem that tells that tale.

For two lengthy sojourns in Romania I am grateful to writer and film director Ted Nicolau who was making some children's films for Paramount Pictures, and the Walt Disney Organisation. The first visit was for a period of four months just after the collapse of the Ceaucescu regime, when visible scars of the coup were very much in evidence—bullet-riddled buildings, shrines with wooden crosses and candles marking where victims had fallen—all the horrors of civil conflict so familiar to ourselves. Despite that initial shock, I have fond memories of many friends made in that lovely country, and I was fortunate in being able to travel fairly extensively, and to pick up at least a feel for the language, which derives directly from the ancient Latin of Trajan's Dacia Felix, later to become the place of exile for the Roman poet Ovid. I would particularly like to thank two young graduates of Bucharest's university for initiating me into something of their country's history through the writings of Nicolae Iorga, introducing me to the poetry of Mihai Eminescu, and the works of Mircea Eliade, Emil Cioran, Constantin Noica, Lucian Blaga, and many others; I was aware already of the plays of Ionesco and the Paris studio of the great sculptor, Brancusi. Jeni Zanfir opened my eyes and ears first in downtown Bucharest, where she and I, together with Michael Higgins, mingled with the vast crowds of an Orthodox Easter to hear the Patriarch announce to the silent multitude: "Christ is risen." She likewise enhanced visits to the palace of Sinaia, the castle of Bran, the Black Church at Brasov, and the mediaeval citadel of Sighisoara. In the grounds of the palace of Mogosaia, behind a wall, I came across an enormous and freshly uprooted statue of Lenin lying beside a smaller one of the first post-war puppet leader of the Romanian state. Sorina Barna was my guide in Sibiu and Rasinari; then down the valley of the river Olt to Rimnicu Vilcea, Cozia monastery, and finally across to the ancient capital Curtea de Arges with its churches, palaces, ancient frescoes, and the curious Fountain of Manole, which commemorates a master mason who fell from the top of a church in which he had immured his wife as a human sacrifice I am indebted to Sorina for locating the original site of a famous ballad on the subject, as well as for her constructive comments on my personal version of what is widely regarded as the definitive Romanian folktale—'Mioritza'. I am further grateful that she put me in touch with professor Jon Filipciuc of Iasi University, who sent me additional information on the materials used in the making of the Moldovan shepherd's pipes and varieties of tree that flourish at a certain height on the Carpathian mountains. Many Romanian writers have drawn inspiration from the implications of this pastoral tale, but its quintessence was captured for me in a single line engraved on a wall in the town of Sibiu, whose source I have not tracked down:

Incremenit—atiudinea in fata mortii.
("Stillness—fit posture in the face of death.")

a sentiment echoed by Byron in his dramatic poem, *Manfred.*

> There is a calm upon me
> Inexplicable stillness! which till now
> Did not belong to what I knew of life.

Something of this spirit has helped me to come to terms with the untimely and violent death of my eldest son, Adam, and my version in English of the tale of the murdered Moldovan shepherd lad is a tribute to his memory. It is dedicated to his mother Beth, his sister Amanda , and younger brother, Hugo, and their families, whose lives were changed forever by the tragedy, as was mine.

It would be less than honest of me I think, not to acknowledge the painful split from my first wife, Beth, and its impact on our young family as yet another manifestation of domestic flight. Time, mutual understanding and love as well as shared loss have done much to draw our extended family closer together. One long affair of the heart followed that break up, and one or two briefer relationships. This period is reflected in certain poems and is part and parcel of an overall picture though not in any biographical sense. In the midst of emotional unrest and instability I met, fell in love with, and married Robina, who for over twenty years now has drawn all the threads of my life together in a wonderful tapestry of domestic happiness without ever once appearing to clip my wings. She has healed old wounds and moved to reconcile old differences, been a tower of strength and loving support through all life's ups and downs and all my quixotic undertakings, this volume of verse being no exception. Because at last the book seems about to find its way into print it is only right and proper that it should be dedicated to her, for without her unfailing encouragement it would never have seen the light of day. She has listened to some foolish outpourings with all the patience of a Penelope yet been constructively critical, because she is nothing if not honest; some emotional excesses have been avoided, thanks to that honesty. She has been tireless in the tedious tasks of proof reading and corrections of spelling, though latterly I have been on the move and been unable to enlist her help, so remaining errors are due to my carelessness, not hers. Another industrious beaver has been our son Toto, who, amongst other things has initiated me into some of the mysteries of the word-processor, and threatens to make me at least semi computer-literate—an appalling prospect for a confirmed and life-long Luddite! Meanwhile he has been largely responsible for turning my handwritten verses into printed pages, and storing them on discs.

In an earlier reference to a Mount Charles coterie, I failed to mention a prominent member of that set, my cousin Kenneth Jamison. A graduate of the Belfast College of Art, he was, in the fifties, a painter and silversmith who was also an occasional and very fine stage designer. As successor to John Hewitt who proposed him for the post, he became an influential art critic for the *Belfast Telegraph* before moving on to a distinguished career as Director of the Arts Council of Northern Ireland, being awarded an OBE and an honorary doctorate. As teenagers at the Methodist College, he, myself, and fellow-actor James Greene formed a triumverate of 'Alberts' who were hell-bent on setting the world to rights on matters of art, literature, philosophy, and so on. The concept of an Albert is too complex to fully explain. Suffice to say that we later appointed an honorary Albert in the person of the distinguished painter T.P. Flanagan, RHA, PPRUA You may have gathered by now that the concept entails elements of loyalty, conviviality, and long-standing friendship; indeed the original trio are celebrating a joint two hundredth anniversary this year, and with the assistance of T.P. a tricentenary might be envisaged.

I mention all this because during this last twelvemonth, when attempting to give this collection a sense of coherence, my splendid cousin and co-Albert has been an excellent sounding board and constructive critic—checking sources, corresponding and telephoning, indicating avenues of exploration, and even suggesting subject matter. Several items, including the opening sonnet 'Flight' and the descriptive piece 'Names' were written at his instigation and in his house, as are these opening remarks. I am grateful to both him and his wife Joan for both encouragement and hospitality.

Finally, my gratitude is due to all those lively folk who contribute so much making the John Hewitt International Summer School the memorable and stimulating experience it invariably is. They are far too numerous to mention by name, but the knowledgeable and kindly director, Dr. Cathal Dallat is a father figure and elder statesman who commands everyone's love and respect, whilst his tireless assistant Hazel Armstrong and her ever-smiling and hard-working staff ensure we are all comfortable, and completely at home.

The troubles of the last thirty years are of course reflected in some of my verses, but after the tragedy of Omagh I have no trite words to add except my sympathy and sorrow, and my profound sadness. I would like some lines of twelve year old Sean McLaughlin who lost his life in that carnage to speak for me and for us all:

> Scatter the seeds of peace over
> our land
> So we can travel
> Hand in hand across the bridge
> of Hope.

James Ellis
Cottingham
Nottinghamshire
October 1998

FLIGHT
for Vincent McInerney

To fly—in the face of Providence,
Of Fortune, or of Danger; to defy
The force of gravity, or simply fly
Into a rage—is ample evidence

Of a richly complex form of parlance:
'Fly man', 'Fly boy', 'Fly by night', 'Dry',
Or 'Spanish' fly; untrammelled 'Flights of fancy'
That transcend earthly circumstance.

A 'Flight of Stairs', 'Locks on a canal',
A 'Dart accessory'—these may seem banal—
But other definitions throw up pearls:

'Oat husk'. 'A cover for the coffee berry'.
'Hurdles'. 'A synonym for Falconry'.
'Flights of angels'. A 'Flight' of Irish earls.

INWARD EYE, INNER EAR
i.m. Rowel Friers

Gaunt gantries, factory horns, and born
Again 'Bible thumpers'. Popcorn,
Pokes of sweets, and Blakes body trusses.
High aspirations. Castles in the sky.
Receding tramlines on the inward eye.
Soft, hissing tyres ... of trolleybuses.

Barry's bumper cars and helter-skelters.
Heinkels, Hurricanes, and air raid shelters.
Wailing sirens. The whine of falling bombs ...

***

A flight of geese, unbidden, may appear—
Enchantment for the eye, as for the ear—
Or Flea Circuses; or fine-toothed combs:

The private microcosm is a dream—
Things are not what they are, but what they seem—
Juxtapositions are at fearful odds
With likelihood and plausibility:
The key to this universe may lie
In cocoa, castor oil, or senna pods.

AFRICAN PROVERB

Don't fly with ducks—you end up getting shot!

MICHING MALICHO

Malicho's a mystery, its meaning lost in history,
But 'miching' was a form of flight, in which the schoolboy
    took delight—
A rooted boyhood institution, despite the dreaded
    retribution—
For freedom was a great attraction, outweighing corporal
    correction!

THE CAT'S WHISKER
in memory of my father

Aye, you'd come racing back, right enough,
You weren't in such a hurry out, the mornings;
Then was it any wonder! Dark classroom,
Dingy blackboard, chalk, the threatening cane—

Public Element'ry? Public Lavat'ry
More like—white tiles, draughty corridors,
Stinging hands from penal slaps on cold
And frosty mornings; sums, the ten-times table.

And yet the brain retains that Yorkshire water-
shed—Swale, Ure; Nidd, Wharfe; Aire, Calder, Don—
And likewise ... '*Constantinople*'—try
Singing 'Con-stan-tin-ople ... '

(The sound of children's voices chanting
'CON-STAN-TIN-OPLE—C—O
—ENNESTY—A—WENTEE—EYE-ENNO—
PEE-ELL-EE' then a swishing cane.)

Day after day those three elusive R's—
Reading, Writing, and A*rith*-ma-tic
Were battered in by rote, by rule, by rod:
Treading the dreary path our fathers trod.

First fist-fight, smashed-up face; the silent trip
With Da to *Woolies*; a cheap punchball and gloves—
Contraption strung from scullery door to floor
'*Left. Left* hand. *Straight* son, *straight*. That's it.'

'Hit *through* the ball, don't tap it. Same again.
Now keep your guard up! Attaboy! That's why
The ball swings back and clouts ye! Slip inside it,
Catch it on the rebound. Right. Right cross.'

Before this, lodged in one childhood memory cell,
I see the Magic Crystal Wireless Set—
Some five to six weeks in the making, this—
The headphones, the mysterious 'Cat's Whisker'.

The final race against the clock—my father
Poised to make contact with America—
'I think the job's a good 'un,' at last, he said
'And now if the lad is early in his bed,

'I'll rouse him and we'll share a bit of history.'
'You'll do no such thing,' my mother said—
I scarpered up the stairs without a word,
Not waiting for the outcome of this tussle—

In the small hours, strong arms lifted me:
'Hush son, me and you is going to learn
Who's to be champion of the world—the Brown
Bomber? Or the miner's son from Tonypandy?'

Fifteen rounds of slogging, and Tommy Farr
Lost on points. 'Robbed, he was robbed,' my father
Growled—I couldn't fathom how he knew—
I only knew, and *know*, that this was true.

'TILLY'
in memory of my mother

How shall I list her skills? She played piano
Dreadfully, but with panache—a certain
Captivating smile or downright belly-
Laugh drowning the worst bum notes—but then
She'd never had a lesson, and, besides,
The thing was out of tune. She would write
Verses that never scanned—well hardly ever.
The rhymes were 'approximate', but if
A sentiment cropped up that shattered 'rules',
She'd soldier on regardless, like McGonagle.

She left school at eleven, but could read
Well, if a trifle slowly. Her handwriting
Took two forms. First, the frenzied scrawl,
To catch quicksilver thoughts, then the fair copy,
School pen dipped in inkwell for copperplate
Results—neat, well-spaced and legible.

And she could count, where it really counted, in
Her head—no huckster ever pulled a stroke
On her—and she could bargain, bid at auction,
Outsmart an Arab in his own bazaar;
Or charm a suit of clothes from a Variety
Market Man. 'Saville Row,' she'd boast,
'Hardly worn and not a mark on it.
I gave the man a ten-shilling note; but
Got my fare home and the price of a fowl ...'
Oh, she was shameless!

            Now there's another thing,
When needful she could wring a chicken's neck,
And yet she had to steel herself each time,
For truly she pitied every living thing;
Nor would she hurt a household fly; but Death

She had no fear of—she laid out bodies, washed,
Scrubbed and straightened them—this a service
For her neighbour ... 'Labour of Love...'

'I know that my Redeemer liveth,' was her Credo,
And on that subject she could quote you chapter,
Verse, jot, and tittle—*commas did not
Escape her*—'Verily I say unto you today ...'
Comma—'Thou shalt be with me in Paradise'.

TO SCUMBLE

Scumble: now there's a word to conjure with,
To call your bluff—marbling, graining, signwork
With serifs—Billy Taylor was a *Master*
Grainer, and then some—cunning and craftsman-
ship his hallmarks—but if you stood around
To watch him work his oracle; his nitty-
gritty, long-nailed *private* mystery—
'Take a wee walk,' he'd say. 'I have to
Concentrate.'—McKelveys were grainers, Frank
Of that ilk a famous man of course. Then there was
Johnny Douglas—but that goes back a long way—
All dead now, you understand, their tradesmen's
Tricks and secret skills gone to the grave.

But living casualties there were, the brown-stained
Mouth of your shellac-drinker, hooked
On varnish, gas-poker addicts, and imbibers
Of a brew of boiled, starched stiff collars—
Then that's all moonshine to a modern wino,
Or trendy teenage glue-inhaler! Those were the
Days my friend, we thought they'd never end.
But end they did; gone, all gone forever.
Sam McKelvey, a quiet man, sparked off
This stream of consciousness, harking back
To happier times—sky not made of stone.

My mother's nail, deformed in a mill mishap
Was narrow like a claw. Her bits of rag,
Sponges, brushes, odds and ends, were kept in a
Hidden drawer. *She* could marble, *she*
Could grain; and *she* could scumble.

PICTURES IN THE FIRE
'There's a child among ye, takin' names'—Robert Burns

Praise be to God for chimleys: pots, pieces,
Stacks, breasts, and cowls; with lum-reek trailing
Clouds of wonder, the inner eye unfailing.
Uncles, cousins, nephews, aunts, nieces,
Assemblies, long gone, round dying embers—
The brain's befuddled, yet the heart remembers
Family resemblances of kith and kind,
A semblance of song ... cloves, clay pipes, *Swift* matches;
Seed cake, scones and soda bread in batches
From the griddle; riddles for the mind—
      Pictures in patches—

For better, worse, memory which serves us, right,
Or wrong—storehouse of being, well-spring
And fountainhead, recording and recounting
Sounds, odours, touch, taste, sight;
Yet fallible as flesh, and prone to error—
Sustaining the ego, distancing the terror;
Transgressions of omission and commission;
Image unstable; a face that lacks a name,
A wrong, half-remembered, without shame,
Rose-tinted spectacles for poor transmission—
      Recall without blame—

Then, what of present mirth, and present laughter:
Science, it seems, favours the godless nation—
The random 'Bang' against the planned 'Creation',
'Here and Now' vis-a-vis 'Hereafter'—
Instead of hearth and home there's central heating,
A better lifestyle, no fairy tales, no cheating—
Meanwhile, the infant's clear, uncluttered brain
Adjusts to all the new technology,
Ingesting a computerised theology,
Sifting through the bones for what remains—
      Child taking names—

[35]

NAMES
for Kenneth Jamison

'Belfast, devout and profane and hard ...

This was my mother city, these my paps,
Country of callous lava cooled to stone,
Of minute sodden haycocks, of ship sirens' moan
Of falling intonations ...'

—Louis MacNeice

Soft 'ciddy-centre' street names—Rosemary,
Fountain, Lombard, Waring, Winetavern;
Castle *Place*, CornMARKET, Arthur *Square*.

Proprietary passages—Crown *Court*, Wilson's,
Hamilton's; Joy's, and Pottinger's *entries*;
Exchange *Alley*; Church *Lane* Upper, and Lower.

Very *public* houses like the Washington;
Private haunts—White's Tavern, Kelly's Cellars;
The Capstan, Morning Star, and Monico.

***

Old entertainment houses, long defunct—
Empire, Alhambra, May's Music Hall;
The Hippodrome, and the Panopticon—

Theatres Royal—marks one and two—
Sarah Bernhardt, Mrs. Siddons, Irving,
Martin Harvey; Chaplin, and Little Titch.

Five soft-sounding departmental stores—
Robb's, Arnott's, Anderson McAuley;
Bank Buildings, Robinson & Cleaver.

***

Unassertive pugilistic forenames—
Rinty, Bunty, Dave Boy, Barry—even
The hard-knuckle hard men sounded

No more threatening than Desperate Dan—
Silver, Buck Alec, Stormy Weatherall;
A nickel, a dollar bill, a Gershwin tune—

Hard-soft city, (rhymes with 'piddy') firm
'Vowls', an' muted *'consonands'*; and Louis's
Aversion for our falling intonations.

***

Hard-line 'gheddoes' of long standing—Sandy
Row, and Divis; the Shankill, and the Falls—
With aitch, stroke haitch a loaded consonant.

Hard-nut fanatics and light-headed bigots
See only hard and fast denominations—
There's even subterranean colour-coding

Where sewage teams clock on as 'green' or 'orange'
Beneath a city cradled by its mount'ns,
Whose 'Fount'n Street' was once The Street of Fountains.

YOUNG PYGMALION
for Patrick McCarville

Stately lady strolls down
Bradbury Place—pillbox
Hat with veil, navy

Costume, calf-length skirt—
What calves! Perfect posture,
Stylish.

Lanky lad crosses
Shaftesbury Square—callow
Youth, twenty; rain

Pissing down—trips and
Falls arse over tit, flies
Through the air with greatest

Ease as from trapeze arms
Round her knees sprawls where he
Falls.

Sorry missus let me
Help ye—gawd yer costume's
Splattered—have I hurt ye?

Couldn't help it legs just
Left me. That is quite all
Right young man; kiss my

Hand and tell your friends you
Fell upon a star—'Miss'

GYPSY ROSE LEE

***

Stately lady strolls on
Stage; behind a screen re-
moves one glove then the

Other—waist, hips,
Thighs, calves—what calves!
Statuesque.

Pygmalion up in the
Gods adores his statue from
Afar but once more trips and

Falls head over heels as
Statue peels layer after
Layer till all's revealed—

Who's to know this is a
Private show—that very
Morning

He'd held her close—a rough embrace—couldn't help it
Didn't plan it legs just

Left him: 'That's quite all
Right young man; kiss my
Hand and tell your friends you

Fell upon a star'—Yours
Most Sincerely—'Miss'

GYPSY ROSE LEE

CLAUSTROPHOBIA
for Graham Reid

'As Our Lord says ... and I agwee *with Him ..*

The initial seeds of claustrophobia,
Fed and watered by excess of love,
And childhood intimations that God above
Had been a personal friend of Queen Victoria;

A royal, loyal, cloying euphoria
That walked, so to speak, hand in glove
With the Divine, first prompted me to move;
For to rebel was anathema.

The overriding sense of rectitude—
Ulster is right, first, last, and all the time;
The fundamental certitude of everything,
The moral, and ethical beatitude—

Then I read somewhere, in a foreign rhyme:
One must not be more loyal than the king!

***

An obvious rider ... someone may wish to add:
Be not more self-righteous than your God!

GOSPEL TRUTH
in memory of Sam Thompson

Saint Anne's Cathedral, Glengormley Gospel
Hall, TUESDAY NIGHT AT THE CRESCENT—'Lessons
In Living from the Book of Judges'—Merciful
Heaven, Ma and Pa were wedded there
In the year of Our Lord nineteen hundred and twenty!

Tomorrow, Messrs. Allen and Hutchinson speak
At Bloomfield Gospel Hall; At Whitehouse, Leslie
Wells of Canada preaches the Gospel of Christ;
The Ulster Temple, Ravenhill, features
George Miller—'International' evangelist.

Whitewell's 'Metropolitan' church has special
Guests—Sydney and Lily Murray; the Church
Of God, Glenmachan Road is 'A friendly sort of
Evangelical Pentecostal Church'—
The Belfast Bible Belt is nothing if not

Friendly; and inventive! Bethany Hall,
Emmanuel, Ebenezer, Elim; Iron
Hall, Assemblies of God, Apostolic,
Christadelphian, Christian Science—and
There's more—Jimminy Cricket! Brethren—'Plymouth

And Exclusive'; Jehovah's Witnesses—
'One foot in the door'—Seventh Day
Adventists—'Signs and Wonders'—Mormons in pairs;
Baptists, Congregationalists. Wesleyan—as in
John—Methodist, free and orthodox.

Presbyterian, Unitarian, Trinit-
arian, Predestinarian; Lutheran—good old
Martin!—Moravian, Disestablishmentarian.
At Central Hall, Mrs. Ewings: Christian
Spiritualism—ADDRESS AND CLAIRVOYANCE.

[41]

This seems to throw another light upon
Sectarianism—Not a Catholic in sight!
These are all aspects of Reform—and yet
There's little concord in the forms of worship:
Who houses, then, the Lord's Peculiar People?

ROME

Like to that fertile goddess, as her chariot sways,
Twin tower-capped coronet trailing clouds of glory, earth
Resounding to her cries—she who to gods gave birth—
So, this teeming city in her Halcyon days

Mothered illlustrious men, more than the Phrygian queen
Herself, men who in turn became as gods, and whose
All-conquering empire vanquished what and whom it
    chose;
Such might as never was, and never *will* be seen

Again! Then, only Rome could Rome herself resemble;
Rome, and Rome alone, cause Rome to quake and tremble.
And so Divinity decreed none should gainsay

Her sole dominion, nor her worldly mandate share: She
Who with Mother Earth held full and sovereign sway. She
Whose God-like valour, moved the gods to dare!

from 'Antiquities of Rome' by Joachim du Bellay

THREE AERIAL SONNETS
for James Greene, Desmond Kinney and T.P. Flanagan

I
Sweeney
'Birth, and copulation, and death
That's all, that's all, that's all, that's all.'
—T.S. Eliot

Sweeney Astray, Sweeney Agonistes,
Sweeney on a hilltop, or a cloud;
Sweeney silent, or embarrassingly loud,
Among nightingales, or other winged species.

Sweeney set to play the part of Icarus—
Feathers preened, inordinately proud—
Or anonymous among a teeming crowd;
Or centred, at the crossroads of the mysteries.

Sweeney as a tribal name on Achill,
Inured to copulation, birth and death—
A clan of consequence in days gone by,

That intruders from the mainland feared to tackle—
For long before the Saxon gods drew breath,
The Lord of Sweeney taught himself to fly.

II
The Heavenly Hiker

'To be able to rise, to be able to fly ... ' 'Ah, yes,'
Thought Beranger, 'What a desirable goal—
To have the facility to take a stroll
In the air, is surely ultimate blessedness'—

For such a gift, would we not give all we possess,
Resort for our bodily needs to the begging bowl,
Dare, like Faust, to pledge our immortal soul
For the pleasure of floating on airy nothingness.

Would weightlessness defy time's tyranny
Or highlight its remorseless irony?
For Beranger, wisdom followed induction:

Back on earth, and bogged down by despair,
What had he seen beyond the troposphere?
Infinite worlds, orbiting to destruction ...

III
Baudelaire
'L'immense clavier des correspondances'

Baudelaire as art critic, was
Outspoken and articulate—lucid, clear—
A voice the mediocre learned to fear,
And not dismiss as a reviewer, because

He understood the visual and its laws,
And championed convictions he held dear—
Modernity, Naïvety appear
Not as pointers, but as clarion calls—

'Partial, passionate, political ... '
'Evocatory witchcraft', 'Intimacy'—
Riots of colour! Assaults upon the senses!

Projections of the physical and spiritual—
Visionary frissons, and soaring flights of fancy,
Upon the vast keyboard of correspondences.

DOMESTIC FLIGHT
*'The street drowns
in Tomatoes.'*—Pablo Neruda

Sod off shadows. Nod off. Doze—
drowse at thirty thousand; dream
of the soft look—

   'Chocolates. Cigarettes. Ice Cream.'

Cock-a-doodle-doo! Cock-a-doodle-doo!

   'Angels and ministers of grace ...'

Click-clack; shuffle; squeak ... and so on.

   'Get thee to a nunnery.
   Why wouldst thou be a breeder ...'

Cock-a-doodle-doo!

Pathe at Mountpottinger—
The Great White Picturedrome,
And that inscrutable stone—

       'Some say ...'
(This is your captain speaking ...)

       'The bird
of dawning singeth all night long ...'

(Turbulence. Seat-belts. Safety exits
Estimated flight time ...)

   'No fairy takes, nor witch hath power to charm ...'

(Isle of Man. River Mersey.
Average drowsing speed—chink!

Glug-glug—'Drink, sir? Ice? Tea
or coffee, madam?')

    'Why seems it so particular ...
    Nay, it is. I know not 'seems'.'

Jean Simmons. Eileen Herlie.
The noble lord and player king—
The late lamented hologram
And quite chop-fallen Archie: 'Alas!'

    'Alas, poor Yorick ...'

                intones in tune with
Bailey's bacon slicer:

              'Now might I
do it pat, now he is a-praying ...'

                  ('How are the mighty ...')

Colvil Street is sound asleep,
The Hillfoot Hustler counts his sheep;
The sunken eyes within their sockets
Envisage breaks, and well-filled pockets;

'Brown'—crack—'Good shot!' 'Green'—
Bright pools, and shadows deep,
With chinks of light and dancing dust:
Click-clack; shuffle; squeak ... and so on—
'Chalk. More chalk ...'

             Long legs, long hair

In Sinclair's shop, and the boy is only eleven—
The child is taking names, I tell you—
'Dan! Where are you, Dan? And Davy?
Will someone play 'Progressive' with this prodigy?'

[47]

A green, a pink, a treble blue,
Extends the break to forty two—

'A marker, Dan! Find the boy a marker'—

   'Pilgrim soul' ... moments of glad
   grace—

       (cover your face with the mask
and breathe normally ...)

                    Dan
Is brewing up the burnt black teapot,
Dragging his ball and chain through streets
Awash with ripe tomatoes—fifteen
To the triangle—smash!
Watch the white—in baulk and tight
Against the cush—

                 ah, Dan's long gone
And Davy, too; gone to shadows deep and
Sunless sepulchres; to fields of poppies—
Yellow, green, brown; blue pink black—
Neruda's nodding butterflies
And bright red, over-ripe tomatoes
In multiples of fifteen, reduced
To pulp and oozing down Park Avenue—
The effluence of half a nation
Heading for the Pumping Station;
The blood and gore of bitter troubles
Recycled as obnoxious bubbles—

'Connswater, Connswater,
Nothing stank like Connswater.'

So, what's the tale behind the stone?
And who, or what, was Pottinger?

[48]

I peer into a smoke-filled den ...

'Play one, Snowy, and eat the rest'—

(The hooded eyes, the lighted fag—
Solo whist, or three card brag—
Cronies huddled over cards,
As reticent as ancient bards.)

I see a war—in truth, a shameful
String of nauseous Opium Wars
Sir Henry 'P' cuts a dash,
And settles their Oriental 'Hash,'
Confounding all their knavish tricks
By striking one resounding 'Six'—
Setting up the Hong Kong lease
To underpin the shaky peace—
Appointed its first governor, too,
In eighteen hundred and forty two:

'GOD SAVE THE QUEEN!'

'A downright con,' says Uncle John,
Who plays a mean game of mah jong,
And is, among his clannish kin,
A little local mandarin—

(The old colonial pattern,
from Hastings to Mountbatten,
from Pottinger to Patten.)

'What price Ulster now?' he cries,
''Midst all the double-talk and lies—
Must we await its swift demise?
Horse-trading and compromise
Seems such a pointless exercise;
And civil strife and revolution

[49]

Have provided no solution—
'Peace' is just another fable
For those who won't sit round a table'—

(So much we learn from history:
The stone retains its mystery ...)

Through murky windows
The light is Whistler's
'Crepuscule at Valparaiso'—
A sombre, grey-green, twilit
Seascape
With tints of mauve and orange,
Vermilion, and deep purple;
'Valpo' of the stairs and endless
Footsteps;
Of old salts in Du Barry's bar

Dreaming of long-dead senoritas,
As Stanley Spenser's wayward brother
Plays serenades for Latin lovers.

Young Pablo lounges in a wicker chair—
A curled up insomniac, hemmed in
By sleeping camaradas—

Tears of passivity, negation—
A watery disintegration,
Foundering in vapour, drowning in

A vacuum

Isolated among unstable

Elements. Oblivious

Of distance or direction

He sinks into the grey-green sea
Beneath the nebulous waves—

The silver whale groans
And wallows—each individual

Jonah

Passively awaits
Regurgitation—

A metallic clunk. A heave.
A jolt. A sound of locking
As of a dungeon door:

('My hair is grey, but not with years,
    Nor grew it white
    In a single night ...')

A whirring noise—flaps lowered—
Pickers and stealers! Spoilers and ailerons!

Not yet! Not yet! Another spasm—
A sense of imminent birth; a breaking
Of the waters ...

And weightlessness—

Gramercy!
Madre de Dios!
The whale has fallen through
The ocean bed, and verily

DANGLES

Patent metamorphosis:
Titanic fins are giant wings
Flapping—Leviathan is

[51]

THE ALBATROSS

Soaring above an astonishing nocturne—
Trills, arpeggios, grace-notes, runs;
All visual—James McNeill ... not Chopin
Or Irish Johnny—

'D'YE KEN JOHN FIELD?'

(Hold on to your hats! The captain is wishing
To shoot a let down: brace yourselves;
Seatbelts securely fastened—no holding
Or stacking; he has clearance—due to
Severe crosswinds and wet tarmac
It will be a hard landing.)

                         'Holy
Mary, mother of God, pray for us
Sinners ...'

            (It's all in the mind of course.)

Receding lines of fluorescence
Vanish to infinity—
Seatbelt signs and icy calm
Induce intense concentration

LANTERN SLIDES FOR DROWNING AVIATORS

Nabney's windows. Three brass balls.
A marble-pillared Orange Hall.
An Iron Mission grim and grey.
A drab red-brick Y.M.C.A.
The Royal Antedeluvian Order
Of Buffaloes—over the road from Lord Street—
Pottinger's Mount. The Short Strand;
And over the bridge, a marching band—

'Terrible as an army with banners ...'

Unwanted tonsils. Bright red
Rubber bib. Ice cream.
Hot water bottle. Scarf
Across the mouth. No trams
To Gawn Street. Paternal piggy-
back. Selected Holy
Pictures; nothing crude
Or vulgar. Holman Hunt—
No relation of Berkeley—
'The Light of the World.' 'The Scapegoat.'
'Behold I Stand at the Door.'

'Knock. Knock.' 'Who's there?'

Sermons. Sermons. Endless sermons—
'In the Temple' or 'On the Mount.'

'Thou art Billy and upon this rock ...'

What's this? The Raft of the Medusa!

'Avaunt, and quit my sight!' 'God's wounds!
Gadzooks! And, by the Mass ...'

Eternal Father. Seamen's Mission.
An upper room in Bradbury Place
That reeked of sanctity and stale

Piss!

An unnerving flapping of angels' wings
As Barry plays the 'Emperor,'
Glen Miller the 'Moonlight Serenade'—
Why does 'Blitzkrieg' spring to mind?
Heinkel, Junkers, Dornier—the Ropeworks

Rivals Dante's *Inferno*, Hillfoot
Street is ablaze from end to end,
Bridge Street is flattened—the *Athletic Stores*
Rased to the ground—Percy Street
Is blown to 'Kingdom Come' as Jimmy
Plays his Magic Flute and trips
The light fantastic. Now, utter
Disorientation—

'THE END IS NIGH.'

Increased speed. Rising tension.
Impaired hearing. Loss of height—
The ground rears up and that's a fact—
Gone is that weightless sense of flight:

GREY GRASS. TICKY-TACKY. TARMAC. IMPACT.

The ground is struck aggressively—
The skipper lands with some panache—

Communal exhalation of breath,
Enough to throw up fifty Jonahs;
Reverse thrust of engine power—
Another hundred Jonahs heave
As white knuckles grip the arm-rests—

('Bla-bla ... Control Tower ...')

Taxi ... taxi ... interminable taxi ...

('Murmur, murmur ... remain seated
Till the aircraft has come to a standstill, and
The engines have been switched off—thank you
For choosing to fly')

'For choosing to fly ... for choosing to fly ...'

OVER THE BRIDGE
for Paddy Devlin

I crossed a bridge and thought to shake the dust
From off my feet, but it was not to be;
For though I fled across the Irish Sea,
Nursing resentment and profound disgust

That individuals had betrayed their trust
And held the public stage in ignominy,
Events o'ertook the ancient enemy,
And time has mellowed memory, as it must.

Homeward I crawl, a wretched prodigal,
To bide awhile, and then again depart—
To leave once more, once more to feel bereft—

Your picture album in my mental holdall,
The hills of Antrim etched upon my heart,
For truth to tell, I never really left.

BLAST
for Tom Gray

Dear Tom, you told me once, quite diffidently,
In your roundabout, off-hand kind of way,
How you walked into a student bar one day,
Bought your pint and sat down, casually

Acknowledging your neighbour's proximity;
Without warning, that world was swept away—
You said you thought you were about to say
'Your health'—but then a bang, a flash, an eerie

Silence and dust; the hand that held the glass
Hovered, inches from your lips; the drink
Had vanished—you said you counted fingers, I think:

'All present and correct'—then, alas,
One glance told you your neighbour's legs had gone;
Only then, did the sense of carnage dawn ...

DOMESTIC

Pertaining to the household, or the home;
Not wild, as in animal, but tame—
One who shoulders duty, takes the blame,
A sober, self-effacing garden gnome—

No jaunts to the stately pleasure dome—
This creature's on a leash, he plays the game;
Thriving on persecution, guilt and shame—
'N'er to wander, never more to roam!'

It lives in Beckett's world of the absurd,
Incurs Cioran's wrath—'The timeless peasant
Enamoured of his torpor'—servile from birth!

Yet in the book that scholars call 'The Word'
This creature's destiny is rather pleasant ...

'The meek shall inherit the earth.'

SUPPER AT SEVEN
for Sir Harry Secombe

As scenes from my childhood unfold in my mind—
Long hours by the seaside, whole days on the sands—
There's grey rocks, and white horses, a wild sky behind,
A stretch of dark shore where a tall pine tree stands;
Across the broad ocean, the dim Scottish hills,
Above me loud seabirds with bright orange bills;
And there's twelve hours of freedom till supper at seven—
Sure, there's fish in the water, and God's in his heav'n.

Beyond in the glen, a great cataract roars,
Over rocks, and round pebbles, the stream struggles free,
As, high overhead, the gaunt cormorant soars—
It will carve out a course to the beckoning sea—
But the sun's barely risen, the day's just begun,
The dog's at your feet and right ready to run;
And the world is your oyster, and God's in his heav'n,
And the time is your own until supper at seven.

Now evening draws in, through you don't feel the cold,
But the dog is dog-tired, and you're nigh on your knees;
And it's time to return, like the sheep to the fold,
By the scent of the sea-wrack that's borne on the breeze.
As you round the last bend you're in sight of Aunt Jean's,
And you catch that aroma of bacon and beans—
Yes, you're right on the nail for your supper at seven,
All's well with the world—and God's in his heaven!

CHILD GODDESS

A childlike beauty of fifteen fragrant years,
Locks of gold in many a ringlet curling,
Soft, blushful cheek—a young maid's colouring—
A smile that sweeps your spirit to the stars!

Matching these looks, Virtue's innocent air—
A snowy neck, a milk-white breast, harbouring
A heart full-fledged in ample bosom burning—
So, Beauty Divine in human form appears.

An eye empowered to turn night into day,
A soft caress to brush all care away—
My soul encapsuled in that heavenly hand—

All this engulfed in transcendental song,
Now soft and plaintive, now smiling, sweet, and strong:
With such enchantments, my reason was unmanned!

after Ronsard

DOLORES OF CARRIGEENBOY

Dolores McDermott is lovelier far
Than your proud painted beauty or fine fillum star

    She's the pride and the joy
    Of Carrigeenboy,
    And of Sligo's sweet town
    The chief jewel and crown.

Now, I have heard it said, a plain girl from the Liffey
Can doll herself up to look grand in a jiffy,
But I tell you, my boys, you may seek far and wide,
Before you'll find better than Garravogue's pride.

By the shores of Lough Skean this young maiden was raised,
And even in childhood her looks they were praised,
As she grew in beauty 'neath soft Sligo skies
She became, of her townland, its treasure and prize.

At the Geevagh crossroads—Michael Peter's oul' place—
All the boys that come in know Dolores' sweet face;
There is Mark, there is Martin, there's Patrick, and John,
With Josie the Fluther, and all the Flynn's Men

And if ever you're passing through old Ballyfarnan—
Sure there's no better venue to stop for a yarn in—
Just ask them straight out who's their pride and their joy,
They'll reply, "Tis Dolores of Carrigeenboy!'

A mile down the road is O'Carolan's grave—
As you pass, raise your cap, or just give him a wave—
By the side of Lough Meelagh he takes his long rest,
The last of the minstrels, and surely the best!

And if he were alive, he would surely hear tell
Of this colleen's sweet nature—her beauty as well—

And, though blind, he would soon the oul' harpstrings
    employ
To praise dear Dolores, of Carrigeenboy ...

Yes, delightful Dolores, is lovelier far,
Than your proud painted beauty, or fine fillum star

    She's the pride and the joy
    Of Carrigeenboy,
    And of Garravogue's town
    The perfection and crown.

***

Now, I'll drop you a hint to put all in perspective:
You may find her, perchance, at the bar of the 'Bective',
Where, if you're a man, or a 'Broth of a Boy',
You may drink to the 'Beauty' of Carrigeenboy—

Yes, Delightful Dolores, is lovelier far,
Than your proud painted beauty, or fine fillum star

    She's the pride, she's the joy
    Of Carrigeenboy,
    And of Garravogue's town
    The perfection and crown.

SONG

Oh love, my love,
How can I tell you
What's in my heart,
What's in my mind;
Though we're apart
Don't be unkind,
My love ...

Was it yesterday
You went away
And never told me why;
And never said goodbye,
My love

(Goodbye my love.)

'Oh, what is deeper than the sea?'
'What lasts through all eternity'—
Affections blowing in the wind,
For love is heedless, love is blind ...

I stand, dear love,
Beneath your window
I dare not sigh,
I dare not moan;
I cannot cry
Though I'm alone,
Dear love ...

Was it yesterday
You went away,
And never told me why
And never said goodbye,
Dear love ...

(Goodbye dear love.)

What came of all those vows we made,
The tender, whispered words we said;
Pledges of undying love
Exchanged beneath the stars above.

Farewell, old love,
I will not follow
Though skies are grey
Now you are gone;
What's there to say,
What's done is done,
Old love ...

Was it yesterday
You went away
And never told me why;
And never said goodbye,
Old love.

(Goodbye old love.)

'Oh, what is deeper than the sea?'
'What lasts through all eternity'—
Affections blowing in the wind,
For love is heedless, love is blind ...

What came of all those vows we made,
The tender, whispered words we said;
Pledges of undying love
Exchanged beneath the stars above.

*Reprise of first thirteen lines of song, then finish with full chorus with
the quatrains reversed.*

What came of all those vows we made,

The tender, whispered words we said;
Pledges of undying love
Exchanged beneath the stars above—
'Oh, what is deeper than the sea?'
'What lasts through all eternity'—
Affections blowing in the wind
For love is heedless, love is blind.

NOUS NOUS TAISONS

Don't let's talk. A breeze disturbs
Two willows by the water's edge;
And I know despite your silence
This evening is the last evening.

Farewell. Leaves are falling. The moon,
Of course, is here—various, patently
Theatrical effects—doves twittering, twilight;
The solitary star, like a full stop.

I sense you catch my half-smile
As in my heart I recollect
A sickly smell of ancient box
Inhaled in old abandoned gardens.

from 'La Verdure Dorée' (1922) by Tristan Derème

N'ANGA N'ANGA
for Paddy

A wise, foolish
Sybil,
A dark-light spirit
Medium—

    'N'anga, N'anga'—

Said there was a
Smell
To Africa, like
Milk.

A subtle musk-like
Odour
Of damp butter
Muslin.

I took the thought
With me
As Aeneus took
The bough—

    'N'anga, N'anga'—

I found no smell,
No stench
Of Africa.
Perhaps

I grow old
And wear
My trouser bottoms
Rolled.

Perhaps I have
Lost ...

(Dear N'anga)

My precious sense of
Smell.

Perhaps—

   'N'anga, N'anga'—

You failed to cast your

Spell.

QUAND VOUS SEREZ BIEN VIEILLE
for Margaret D'Arcy

When you are very old, at evening by a fire
Of dying embers, the candle low, the sewing cast
Aside, oh then, you'll say my lines aloud at last
And cry, amazed—'I was the Muse for Ronsard's lyre;'

'When young and beautiful this face did once inspire
His passion and his pen!' But that's all in the past—
Now, your one companion, a senile servant fast
Asleep beside the distaff, will start awake to enquire

How this 'Ronsard' came to immortalise *your* name—
I shall be beneath the sod, a formless Phantom
Who, in the myrtle shade, seeks peace and quiet rest.

And you? A fireside crone, soured by regret and sorrow—
Grasp hold of love, I say! Don't wait until tomorrow;
Pluck today life's roses, and crush them to your breast.

from 'Sonnets for Helen' *by Ronsard*

FOR JULIA AND STEPHEN'S WEDDING
'Where Lagan steam sings lullaby,
There blows a lily fair ...'

You asked for a poem—that's
a tall order, especially for
a wedding day—the banns are up,
what more is there to say: the die
is cast, desire is mutual ...

The lovelorn lenanshee is held
in thrall and lingers still along
the flower-strewn way where fond and faithful
sweethearts choose to stray: where lilies
blow, and Love is Lord of all.

Where, when you stumble, the hand is there
to hold—falling, you're cushioned by
Love's warm embrace, and rooted
sorrow is mere memory—

Joy is redoubled, unfounded
fear consoled: and doubt is
confronted face to face ... where Lagan's
murmuring stream sings lullaby.

SOLITUDE
for Sorina Barna

At my plain pine table
With curtains drawn, in pensive mood,
Dancing tongues of flame enable
Thoughts to wander as they should.

Images and memories
Crowd into my teeming rhyme,
Like crickets' stilted melodies
Trapped in the masonry of time.

Or, they fall like gentle rain
Upon the casing of my soul;
Or sink, as candles on the wane,
In molten shapes that run and roll.

Around the room in every nook
Spiders weave their webs of silver,
Whilst in and through each dust-bound book,
Soft-footed mice browse and pilfer.

And I gaze up at the ceiling
As I hear their molars grinding,
And their low, contented squealing
As they gnaw through every binding.

Oh, how often have I wished
To lay aside my worn-out lyre—
The strings unstrung, the task accomplished;
A cogent reason to retire—

But then the crickets and the mice,
With their soft insidious tread,
Awake my Muse, in a trice,
And with new verses fill my head ...

Now and then—alas, not often—
When the lamp is burning late,
Suddenly, my heartbeats quicken;
The latch is lifted at the gate!

It is 'Herself'—my dingy room
Is all at once ablaze with light,
As though an icon's golden gleam
Had crossed the threshold of the night.

Time has no meaning now
As heart to heart begins to speak;
And we exchange one loving vow—
Hand in hand; cheek on cheek.

from the Romanian of Mihail Eminescu
Bucharest, 1994

MIORITZA
in memory of my eldest son, Adam (1960-1988)

From heaven's doorstep
Down the sheep tracks
Came three shepherds
With their flocks,
Slowly, slowly off the mountain—

It's the plain truth, not a word of a lie—
A Moldovan, a Magyar, and a Vlach—

And a little snow-white lamb—
God strike me dead—
She moved her lips
And this she said.
Softly, softly on the mountain—

It's the simple truth, not a word of a lie—
A Moldovan, a Magyar, and a Vlach—

'By the budding horns
Upon my brow
Pay heed to what
I tell you now, (baa-aa-agh,)
Plainly, plainly, on the mountain'—

It's the honest truth, not a word of a lie—
A Moldovan, a Magyar, and a Vlach—

'By the snow-white fleece
With which I am blessed,
And by the sun
Low in the west,
Sinking, sinking on the mountain'.

'By God above
Up in the sky

Who knows when all men
Live and die, (baa-aa-agh.)
Surely, surely on the mountain'—

It's the shocking truth, not a word of a lie—
A Moldovan, a Magyar, and a Vlach—

HER SHEPHERD WAS THE MOLDOVAN.

'Oh, little lamb,
Your cheeks are pale,
Are you unhappy,
Or unwell?'

'So loud you bleat
Yet do not eat
What are these words
That you repeat,
Upon the mountain?'

('Baa-aa-agh! The Magyar and the Vlach!')

'Oh, Master dear
I greatly fear
I lately heard them
Plot your death,
On yonder mountain.'

'Rise up now, while
You still have breath,
And run for life
E'er they appear;
E'er they appear'—

('Baa-aa-agh! The Magyar and the Vlach!')

'Oh, little lamb

With fleece of snow,
What you relate
I surely know,
Upon this mountain.'

'But what's to be
Will ever be,
Though I should stay
Or I should flee;
Or I should flee ...'

'But place my pipes
Upon the ground
That when the wind blows
They may sound
Across the mountain—
Oh, when the wind blows
Let them sound,
To rock my sleep
With peace profound,
With peace profound:
One of elder,
One of bone—
The strident, and
The tender tone—
And one of beech
With dulcet drone,
To lull my dogs
When day is done.'

'For though my soul
Depart the clay,
My body in
This earth they'll lay—
I'll greet it as
My wedding day'.

And so the ewe
Began to weep,
Though she was but
A lowly sheep:

And as the teardrops
From her fell
The humble shepherd
Wept as well,
He wept as well—

Not because
His time was come,
But for the lamb
He thought was dumb—

Then thought he of
His widowed mother—
An only boy,
She had no other—
She'd wander through
The mountains wild,
Enquiring for
Her missing child:

'Oh, have you seen
My precious son,
He is the handsome
Moldovan;
His hair is soft
As finest silk,
His skin is whiter
Than the milk;
His eyes, green berries
In the Spring,
His beard, the shining
Raven's wing.'

'Tell not my mother
I am dead;
Say I am
But lately wed,
And that the blissful
Bride and groom
Were sponsored by
The sun and moon.'

Her shepherd boy
Now wears a crown,
And on his back
A golden gown
'His paramour
So fair and fine,
A princess of
The royal line.'

'Presiding priests
Were snow-capped mountains—
Their chant, cascading
Streams and fountains—
Fir, and Spruce,
And Maple tall
Wove the bridal
Coronal.

Feather'd creatures
Of the air
Were flutes and fiddles,
Rich, and rare;
The forest was
A merry throng
Which danced and sang
The whole day long.'

'Say a star
Fell from the east

To shine upon
The wedding feast—
Great constellations
In the sky
Shone their lanterns
From on high.'

'Tell her I will
Send to her
A true and faithful
Messenger;
And she will meet
My lovely bride
And live forever
By our side.'

'Oh, Mioritza
Meek and lowly,
Weep not for me
When I am gone,
When I am gone—
Though life be brief
The end is holy:
And God shall shield us,
Every one—
Yes, everyone'—

('Moldovan, Magyar, Vlach')

'On His high mountain.'

'Ca la nunta mea.' 'It is my wedding day.'

a personal version of a Romanian folktale

SHACKLETON
for Marie, Robina and Toto

Two adjoining television lounges,
One tuned to golf, one to Elvis Presley—
A 'Celebration' of his death, I think—

Curled up forms in foetal postures, others
Stiff as boards, and some with heads lolling—
Silent figures flitting in and out:

Watchful carers, keeping a weather eye—
A twilight zone of sighs and groans, the hollow
Laugh or two, and inarticulate mumblings.

('Creeps in this petty pace from day to day.')

*

By a door stands Bob, absorbed for hours
On end, confronted by its mysteries,
His hips gently swaying to and fro—

The door, for him, a symbol of confinement
And no wonder; himself confined four years
In Changhi Jail, maltreated, starved, and tortured—

And now, this private hell, a cruel echo—
From here, as from himself, there's no escape—
How to get *out*? How to *get* out? *How*?

('Tomorrow, and tomorrow, and tomorrow)

*

Shirley, too young to be in here, and looking
Puzzled, angry, sinks to her knees but not

In prayer—wringing hands as in despair—

She mimes a sweep of circularity—
A scrubbing brush? A duster? Mansion Polish?
Then a convulsive back and forth attack—

A stubborn stain perhaps? She was a cleaning
Lady, renowned for her thoroughness—
A white coat steers her from her futile labour.

    ('Will all the perfumes of Arabia ...' and so on.)

*

Dotty Dancer is too far gone for such
Heroics—not for her, even subliminal
Arabesques, or slippered soft-shoe shuffles.

What happens in the subways of her mind?
A distant drumroll? Vibrato violins?
A swish of velvet and a beam of light?

She partnered Jack Buchanan in her time,
And gathered lilacs with Novello—now,
Her finale shares a stage with Rita Hayworth.

    ('Where are they now, the shows of yesteryear?')

*

Where are they now, the hurricanes and spitfires?
Lancasters, Wellingtons, Ansons, and Shackletons—
'Who said Shackleton? Reporting for duty!'

'Albert William Taylor,' navigator—
'Fingers out!' 'At ease!' The war is over—
Back in Civvy Street, we'll live in clover.

Goodbye Calcutta, farewell Table Mountain—
Hello green fields of France and Merrie England
Salutations, white cliffs of Dover!

('The sea is calm to-night, the tide is full ...')

*

Sweet-faced Bill, not all your dreams came true,
Though memories remain, a sorry few—
There's still a wife to hold your hand, a daughter

To stroke your cheek, a grandson to yell 'PEEP-BO!'
Today, recognition is touch and go—
Hope tries her damnedest to dominate despair—

You recall you had relations, long ago,
Who turned their backs and never saw you go—
Too late now, to call—Hello? Hello?

('Put out the light, and then put out the light.')

LONG HAUL
for Bill Bryden

The first African image

Was not baked earth and indolent
Water. Not absence
Of contour.

Featureless
Bush filtered through
Tropical

Haze.
Not

Buildings
On flat ground. Tacky
Tarmac. Factory chimneys
On Harare's

Outskirts.

Nor cooling towers absurdly
Standing sentinel in drab
Dove-grey gowns. Nor shabby
Suburbs. Nor seedy shanty

Towns.

Nor foregatherings
of white-robed 'Apostles'
At wayside prayer. None

Of these.

The thrust
Was colour:

Vivid. Overriding.
Daubed at random over
Muted greens
And ochres.

Deepest lavender inclined
To regal purple. Majestic.

Intense. Exotic. All-
Pervading. Heady.
Hypnotic. Half-
Hallucinatory and wholly
Intoxicating.

Then vanished
Into air. Into thin

Air.
Jumbo

Heaving his incredible
Bulk across a perimeter
Fence
Thence

Increase of tension. Heightened
Noise. Flaps flapping. Deftly
Poised—tail high, head low.
Straight rudder; deep
Groan; involuntary
Shudder—

   'Hear the mighty engines roar!'

Equilibrium as before:

Full tilt at rising ground.
Ungainly charge. Dainty

Touchdown—

'Hup! Hup!' 'Mumbo

Jumbo ...'

'Thank you, Ladies and gentlemen,
Kindly remain ... '

'Seated ... ' (bla-bla)
'Standstill.' (bla-bla-bla)

'Engines ...
Switched off.' What
A palaver!

The dismal demi-monde
Of airport terminality.
The boredom. The banality.
The backside-of-beyondness.

Dingy crystal maze. Transition
Limbo. 'Neither-here-nor-there-ness'
Nowhere-in-particular-ness—

Indecision. Tunnel vision—

Harare. 'Oh, ho!'

Thought and action freeze in tandem:

    'Currents turn awry ...'

[83]

Brain and body shift at random.
Weight transference. One foot to ...
Another:

'How far to Timbucktoo?' I wonder—

('Shouldn't start from here
Try the other hemisphere.')

A hive of inactivity—
Then, all at once.
A surge
A renaissance
A multiple nativity
As immigration officials
Officiously
Emerge

What's the norm?

Fill in a form
And form a queue:
Routine Q & A.
'Good day!'
You're through—

Where to? Where to?

Amusement Hall and Carousel—
Cleethorpes out of season. Clacton
On a dull day.
Play

THE BAGGAGE GAME.

Fast reactions.
Watch

The action. Grab a trolley.
Snatch.
Then back away
To load up
The belongings
And duty free shop

Things.

MANUAL DODGEMS

Clunk. Thump.
Push. Shove. Bump.
Choose green not red. Embrace
The human tide. Face

THE GHOST TRAIN RIDE.

Not scenes of doom and gloom.
Horror from the days of yore—
Slaves in shackles, four by four—
Not that kneeling figure:
'Death in the attitude of prayer.'—
Livingstone, may one presume!
Not Mary, in delirium
Or Gordon, stranded at Khartoum

None of these:

Reality assumes a spectral aspect.
The blood chills at the awesome prospect
Of normal abnormality—

Hotels. Taxi. Car hire.
Blurred surnames, absurdly
Out of focus.
Weave through teeming

Placards, seeming
Swarms of locusts
Hell-bent on survival.
Assertive predators and pre-
Determined prey,
Paired off on arrival
And swiftly whisked away.

Thus far, this dreary journal blow by blow:
So, this is Africa! Not so. Not so ...

Walk into the light!
And there to greet you—attired
In ceremonial raiment
Behold! The Jacaranda!

A surge of vibrancy,
Of latent power—life
Enhancing, all entrancing
A sight to levitate
The spirit; a quintessential
Sense and soul of Africa—

    'Purple! Royal purple—
    All hail the Jacaranda!'

Hic et ubique—
Here, there, and everywhere
This univeral tree
In brave profusion blooms:
It's not indigenous,
It's from Brazil—who cares!

Whole avenues are lined,
Sinuous limbs entwined
Each around its neighbour:
A divinity of form!

A thing of paradise
Endowed with Eden's plumage!

    'Purple! Royal purple—
    All hail the Jacaranda!'

In this resplendent shade
A humble shrub may shelter:
She blossoms thrice—white,
Speckled, dark madder—
Beneath the Jacaranda,
The royal Jacaranda

Her name is:

    'Yesterday,
    Today, and tomorrow.'

As though to say:

    'SIC TRANSIT
    GLORIA MUNDI.'

Put another way:

    'After joy, comes sorrow.'

Meanwhile, the Jacaranda,
The glorious Jacaranda—

Majestic.
All-pervading.
Exotic
And intense.

Heady.
Hedonistic.

Half-
Hallucinatory
And wholly

Life enchancing—

Blooms on. Blooms on.

   'Purple! Royal Purple!'

   'All hail! All hail!'

'All hail, the Jacaranda!'

TREE STUDIES
for Amanda and John

Gregarious Msasa—the gnarled
Trunk a bowed leg, the upper
Body malformed, the limbs
Contorted, puny, pointed leaves
Affording filtered

Shade—
Covers

Gently sloping inclines
And dramatic outcrops known to Kipling as
'Kopjes'.

Mopane—a very hardy tree,
Bifoliate as a butterfly,
With drooping leaves and juicy pods,
Edible, and browser-friendly,
Offering fragrant

Fodder—
Grows

On dry savannah, veld, and grassland,
And flourishes in poorly drained
Soils.

Flat-crowned Acacias include
Umbrella Thorn and Paper Bark;
Karoo is common, and the prolific
Wattle is alien—
Known associates:

Giraffe.
Leopard—

A nibbler, and a carnivore;
The latter stretched full-length along
A bough.

A presumptuous Eucalyptus, flayed
Like foolish Marsyas—what's left
Of bark flaking, like leprosy:
A leaf, crushed in the palm, exudes
Mortality—

Erect.
Tall.

It stands, defiant as Lobengula,
Head feathers etched against a turbulent
Sky.

Albida, or 'Anaboom', adorns
Zambesi's banks, whilst drought-resistant
Adansonia Digitata—
The hairy titan known as Baobab,
'King of Lowveld'

Is crowned
In Spring

With honey-blossom, invoking Tennyson's
'Murmurings of immemorial
Bees.'

ON THE WING
for Hugo and Rachel

A tawny eagle on the wing
Against a twilit sky; hordes
Of white-backed vultures, hunched on treetops;
A steppe buzzard, standing sentinel,
Sharp eyes on alert for prey—
Novel, awe-inspiring sights;
Exotic visions, in abundance,
Re-animating jaded sense—

At dawn, a long-tailed shrike, stock-still
Upon what seems a slender reed,
Is startling, to say the least:
The curved, uncompromising beak
Belies a song of dulcet beauty—
Nearby a vocal relative
Whose love duets are quaintly eerie;
The green and yellow bokmakerie ...

A malachite kingfisher, streaked
Electric blue, and russet red,
With swordbright beak and ruffled crest,
Hovers by a river bank—
A quivering twig above the water,
A clear reflection in the stream;
He takes off at the speed of light
In dazzling horizontal flight—

Hoop-hooping hoopoes, heard, but seldom
Seen, a glimpse of masked weaver;
A kurrichane thrush with flame-like beak
Foraging freely at my feet ...

***

A tiny paradise flycatcher—
Blue head, white breast, chestnut wings,
Perched outside my window bay,
Quite simply took my breath away—

DESTINATIONS

Evangelina. Figtree.
Concession. Colleen Bawn.
Cashel. Connemara.
Chimoko and Cement.

Fatima. Fort Usher.
Inyani. Chishawasha.
Bambata. Bulawayo.
Masvingo and Mayo.

Troutbeck and Triangle.
Jury. Junction Gate.
Chatsworth. Gutu. Gweru.
Nyanga. Nandi. Nora.

Plumtree and Pambuka.
Victoria Falls. Kariba.
Hwange. Gonarezhou.
Matobo. Leopard Rock.

Avila and Aberfoyle.
Trelawney and West Nicholson.
Battlefields and Bannockburn.
Glenclova and Glenlivet.

THE ROAD TO GLENLIVET
for David Horovitch, Jonathan Firth, and Susannah Harker,
who took the same road—'Tin Man', 'Scarecrow' and 'Dorothy'

Dingy terminals. Dreary lobbies. Dog-eared
Travel bumph ... and maps. Unwieldy maps.

Bromley. Binga. Bonzo. Bumi Hills!

Departures are exhilarating ...

Duchess Hill. Eiffel Flats. Escafe.
Eldorado! To travel hopefully
Is better than

Arrival.
Mere survival ...

    Veni ergo sum

Rotten Row. Belevedere.
Borrowdale. Belgravia!

    Round and round Harare
    Like a teddy bear ...

Find the open road. Who needs
To fly—Mutare. Marandera ...
Masvingo—Bingo! A whiff of euphoria
As we head for Fort Victoria!

On and on over featureless veld—
Mile after mile of monotonous novelty.
Mile after mile of polite disinterest.
Mile after mile—what would we give for a
Herd of buffalo! What would we give for a
Cowardly lion—thank the Lord

For Dorothy, and follow the Yellow Brick Road ...

    Dorothy drives like a wild thing
    Dorothy flies like the wind

Not one heap of balancing rocks,
And kopjes are few, and far between

Beatrice.
Featherstone.
Fairfield ...

We had stopped at a joint called 'Vic's' at Chivhu—
A racy saloon with a single star
That had seen its share of prospectors in days gone by—

Settled by Boers, they had called it

    'ENKELDOORN'

A 'one thorn' town—such mind-blowing

    'Dutchness'—

Ah, well! As Mr. Jingo has it:

    'A kopje is always a kopje,
    And a Boojer is always a Boer.'

Near Chatsworth, a diversion to 'Nowhere
In Particular'—the yellow road
Is brick-red now, a winding strip
Of terra-cotta, that snakes across
The silent bush, that kicks up stones
And dried up stour, that bends, and turns,
Interminably—Dorothy flying

'Like the wind!'

Monkeys! Monkeys everywhere—
Above, below, across our path;
And schools of foraging baboons—
Chatter. Chatter. Cocktail chatter:

    'Cheers, old boy.' 'Chin chin.'
      'Nice weather ...'

Two tall girls with mealie bags
Balanced above shining faces—
Ascot hats of vast proportions
Worn with elegance, and grace—

Slowing down. Slowing down ...
Thatched huts, in a clearing.
Cattle grids—one, two, three—

    Dorothy driving. Dorothy driving ...

Further hints of habitation:
Cart tracks. A small kraal.
Paths diverging, right and left.
A fully-laden donkey. A team
Of oxen, yoked together as in
Bible picture books. A clump
Of trees. A steeple—

    SERIMA MISSION CHURCH

Gleaming white, and solitary:

'Why do missionaries haunt
Such wild, recondite spots?' enquired
The Scarecrow, 'Why do they fly
To the ends of the earth? Are they migratory?'

'Go ye into all the world,'

Said Dorothy—'Well, fair enough!
But what about West Hartlepool?'

There followed a sober silence, as though
To imply, there was no answer to that;
But it must have occurred to us, at the time,
To ask ourselves a similar question ...

The Tin Man was informative:

'Rural skills of scale and substance
Built this place, led by a Swedish
Builder-Priest who much impressed
Evelyn Waugh ...'

    (Ah, well!)

     'It will,'

Said Waugh, 'Compare in years to come,
With mediaeval masterpieces.'

Thus sayeth the dog-eared travel bumph:

NORTHERN CLARITY. AFRICAN
APPLICATION. INHERENT
SHONA ARTISTRY

The architect has left his mark,
But what about the priest? And those
Anonymous artisans ... what about
Poor Evelyn Waugh! No sign of nuns
Or missionary brothers—the building
Spoke for itself—Ah, me!

'This sad vicissitude of things.'

Torrential rain—'Go to Spain'
'Never show your face again!'

    Dorothy driving like the wind—
    'Bless me father for I have sinned'—

Somewhere up there skies are blue—
'Which way now?' 'Bear left for Gutu ...'

Over the level crossing, then,
Follow the Bulawayo line—

    Dorothy driving, on, and on,
    South to Masvingo, and beyond:
    Now we inhale the pure euphoria ...
    As we 'fly' through Fort Victoria!

Suddenly, without forewarning,
The country's changed,

The weather's turning ...

Dorothy still driving

    a scarecrow,

A tin man,

    and one cowardly lion

***

The spirit of Glenlivet was, clearly,
Unconjurable, and yet there was this startling

Déjà-vu-ness

She sat athwart a highland
Glen, her spectral aura
Trailing Gallic vapours, her head
Lost in hazy hills, and at
Her foot, a Caledonian loch—

'Stern and wild.'

Dampness was in the air, scudding
Clouds, uncharacteristic chill—
Manifestly unseasonal mists
For Springtime in the tropics—a sunset
Had been forecast ... Lord! What labour!

A soggy sheet of Cox's grey:
A wash of watered down lamp black
On Prussian blue with just a tinge
Of ochre: above the Beza mountains,
Chrome cracks split the sky—
They turned to smouldering amber, then
To bright blood-orange; yet still the grey
Predominated, still dark rain clouds
Blotted out the sun—but, high,
Wide, and handsomely, pale
Cerulean merged with a deeper hue
Of pure, clear cobalt ...

Slowly, painstakingly, a flush
Of rose madder seeps across
A sodden sky—water, more water—
This artistry outdoes Turner's
Late, liquid landscapes, or Whistler's
Plausible nocturnes—

'I mix my colours with my brains.'

Upper air is points of pink and blue,
Fragile fauna bathe in glistering dew:
Pale, white roses blush for joy,
And moonflowers gape to catch the sun;
Proteas redden, fireballs burn,
Date palms don a purple robe;
Paw-paw, guava, avocado,
Bask in evening's afterglow.
A pink-flowered shrub without a handle
Blazes like a Roman Candle,
As Sol, in regal majesty,
Sinks beneath the western sky.

Out of sight, at Great Zimbabwe,
Buried with the ancient kings,
Long-dead spirit-doctors dabble
In day to day prophetic things:
A local N'anga, or diviner,
Predicts tomorrow will be finer—
Perhaps he's tuned to ZBC,
or saw the forecast on TV.

From John Webb's Bar I'd thought to hear
The skirl of pipes, or Jimmy Shand ...
But no, it's vintage Perry Como:

'Magic Moments'. 'Time Goes By.'

(SLOWLY, OH, SO SLOWLY ...)

'Ah, me! The fleeting years!'

Time for the log fire and the malt—

WHISKY. FINE MALT WHISKY.

SHONA WOMAN
for Jenny Lipman

A Shona woman
Tall
Wearing white to set off
Smooth
Dark
Skin

As a pale
Princess
Might wear a little black
Number
Poised
Chic

Shoulders back
Erect
Breasts thrust forward bottom
Flat
Sheer
Class

Slips a foot
From
A stylish patent leather
Shoe
Toe
Slithers

To and fro
So
Seductively to stroke a
Braced
Shining
Calf

Presently
She
Resheaths her foot with a
Swift
Firm
Thrust

Watching her
One
Thinks of Baudelaire ...

***

Sad
Forlorn
Voyeur

FROM THE GREEK

Epigram

This town's big-bellied, great with child—
She could bring forth a monster—
Oh, your 'man in the street'
Has a titter of wit, but wild men
Hold the reins, he just carries the can.

Inscription I

She came from South Belfast, we called her 'Spot'—
Da says she was the best dog of the lot—
One day she wandered off into the dark,
To roam where we no longer hear her bark.

Inscription II
for Barry McGuigan

This marble statue—erected by grateful opponents
In memory of 'Paddy the Pugilist' who in life
Stood stock-still in the ring, not laying a glove
On any one of us—may he rest in peace.

THE BOTTOM LINE

1

To me, as to many another, she
Is an unkind mistress, promising untold
Delights—transports to the realms of gold,
A Timeshare in the Land of Arcady,

Like minds attuned in perfect harmony,
Vibrant modernity founded upon the old,
A Utopia where nothing tawdry is bought or sold;
A Muse! A Grace! A God, perhaps, for company—

But Inspiration? Ah, no, she has fled:
The dark recesses of the mind are blank,
And absent is the Mother of Invention.

I conjure up the books that I have read—
Master texts, rank on serried rank—
Ironic laughter mocks my good intention.

2

Put another way, I toss and turn
Among bloated corpses in a stagnant pond,
Float sidelong through backwaters of beyond
And crawl beyond a point of no return.

I swim through oceans where great oak trees burn,
Scream in imagined pain yet make no sound,
Fight cats in dustbins on a Merry-go-Round,
And place a stone upon a dead dog's cairn.

So, is there no awaking from this dream?
No remission? No early morning light?
No vision of a future? No tunnel end?

With Schopenhauer, things are what they seem;
The world is his idea, his birthright—
It's not a birthright I would recommend!

3

I turn to Sidney's celebrated Muse:
'Look in thy heart and write'—that's not an option;
Romantic Poetry is dead and gone;
It's with O'Leary,—read the National News—

Forbye, Science would have us disabuse
The mind of self-delusion—the heart's function
Is prosaic; a flawed automaton
Prone to error, breakdown, and misuse;

Nothing to do with feelings or emotions—
Another organ may carry on the job,
Transplanted from a stranger lately dead—

It's time to ditch those old 'heartfelt' notions,
To look on Nature as a soulless blob,
And tear up all those sloppy books you've read.

4

And yet, and yet ... the human heart's a wonder,
If only in a literary sense—
The corpus of her work is immense,
She'll clog a library with blood, and thunder—

Her agonies can tear the world asunder,
Her loyalties are rigid, and intense,
Her gifts, gold, myrrh, and frankincense;
Her erudition? Blunder upon blunder!

[105]

And her lack of common sense is legendary:
But her generosity's a living byword,
Her capacity for love is infinite,

Her selfless courage, quite extraordinary;
And though her want of wit may seem absurd,
She'll fight a losing battle, and then win it!

5

The man is going abroad to provide for his family—
To provide for his fam'ly, the man is going abroad:
If the inversion appears clumsy, or odd,
Try speaking the words aloud as a rhythmic homily:

('The man is going abroad to provide for his family,
To provide for his fam'ly, the man is going abroad.')

The initial utterance puts the case succinctly—
The man *is* departing his native sod
To provide for his family's needs, thanks be to God!
Let's wish him well in his Newfoundland of Plenty.

The inverted word order hints at contingency:
Has the 'Native Sod' been exploited perhaps?
Can the natural habitat no longer provide?

Has the home-bred cow been milked by a foreign agency?
Is the native economy in a state of collapse?
Is oral syntax an unreliable guide?

6

An oppressive silence governs the dead of night
In a city centre; deserted streets are tense

Under a risen moon—raw suspense
Unleavened by augury or human insight—

Is it a prelude to terror, or sudden flight?
Is that a whiff of semtex, or frankincense?
Is this truce a victory for common sense,
Or will one faction invoke a divine right

To let loose unholy mayhem? The ancient Greeks
Unleashed their civic madness with such bloodlust;
They too, had factions, gods, and warring sects,

As zealous as our own sectarian freaks;
Some third millennium Homer surely must
Immortalise our Iliad, its causes, and effects.

7

In fact it is more a Peloponnesian War—
For Athens and Sparta at each others throats,
Read Prod and Taig burning respective boats
Till finally there's nothing left to fight for.

To blow sky high a betting shop or bar,
Preach policies of hatred to win votes,
To see 'Orange Bastards', or 'Fuck the Pope' in quotes
Must tell us something about who we are!

And we perpetuate the stalemate on television
Play Party Games to titillate the Media—
On Question Time it's all a bit of fun—

Is it any wonder we suffer from tunnel vision:
For us, there is no 'Fin de la Comedia';
Like 'The Mousetrap', this show will run and run!

8

And yet, and yet ... the people are astounding,
Their worth and virtues tested in the fire—
Qualities the world can but admire;
Humour and generosity abounding—

That's why the status quo is so confounding.
Has religion really dragged us through the mire?
It is probably bad form to enquire,
For dogma is part and parcel of our grounding.

Yet religious leaders have a dubious record,
Not just here, but all around the planet,
Wherever war and civil strife are raging.

Why don't they all stand up with one accord
And cry 'Enough!' The plain truth is they cannot:
Deep down, it's 'Holy War' that they are waging.

9

What is Holy War? Men defending
Their own perception of Almighty God?
If that is the premise, the argument is flawed—
The Infinite's beyond man's comprehending;

Protecting the All-Powerful is lending
A touch of farce to the concept of Jehad,
Reducing the sublime to the absurd:
There is no beginning, and no ending—

Churchmen and politicians have shifted goalposts
In every generation. Expediency
Is all they preach, or fully comprehend,

With few exceptions—the mortal soul posts
Its parting testament: if the quality of mercy
Is not strained, it must hope that the Almighty
understands.

10

The Clergy! Well frankly, I feel sorry for them
They are either sleek, well-appointed bishops
With stabilising ballast amidships,
Or they're thin with reedy voices full of phlegm,

A protruding Adam's Apple and no diaphragm;
Unlike their bosses, who have sensual lips
An easy delivery, and child-bearing hips—
One I see often is a perfect gem—

They're appointed first to what is called a 'Living'.
And truth to tell they often have to earn it—
And all because they're not a 'Son and Heir'—

They can often be aloof and unforgiving,
If they have not charity, they seldom seem to learn it,
And under the Mitre, they sometimes lose their hair!

11

The artist should keep a weather eye on science—
Science and madness have a strange affinity,
One fool with access to just one appliance
Could blow our ageing planet to infinity

Does this sound like a whiff of modern heresy?
No poet could induce such an eclipse,

No mad musician unleash such a fury,
No painter invoke such an Apocalypse!

Thomas Stearns averred there'd be no bang;
He saw the planet ending with a whimper—
I think, myself, that's when the doorbell rang:
No second thoughts—nothing could be simpler!

Beware! A scientific Samson, one day,
Will reach down and uproot the Axis Mundi.

12

'The Bottom Line!' How I detest that phrase
Along with other verbal excrement
'Mugging,' 'Road Rage,' 'Buzz-Word,' 'Non-Event'—
This journalistic crap's become a craze.

A well-fed windbag will win much praise
Proposing a motion in a conference tent.
Or spouting on Private Health, or Man-Management—
The faithful hanging on every word he says:

'It's 'A Nonsense' to demand 'Fair Shares for All,'
'Every man for himself' is our 'Modern Dream'
The 'Buzz-word' for today, is 'Enterprise!'

It's 'A fact of Life' 'The weakest go to the wall,'
'At the end of the day,' 'Fat Cats' must have their cream;
'The Bottom Line' is the nurses don't get their pay rise.'

13

How do I love you? Words cannot convey
The depth of affection, the passionate unrest—

The word itself emblazoned as on a crest
Of gold—L.O.V.E.

The escutcheon, cared for and burnished every day,
Gleams like shining armour on my breast,
Sustaining me through every trial and test,
Guarding a loyal heart right jealously:

But why unrest? Because it seems so fragile,
And human life is tenuous and brief;
Yet I know there is a thread of tempered steel

That binds true lover's hearts and will not fail:
Before that power, I tremble like a leaf,
Hold my breath, bare my head, and kneel.

14
for John and Sherrie Keegan

True lovers transcend space and teems of time
More readily than empires or great kings—
Dynasties are passing, temporal things;
Love survives in breathless tales and rhyme—

Even the lovers in the pantomime
Share endless youth and everlasting spring,
Love makes the world go round, the heart to sing
And shares the Universe with the sublime:

Dante and Beatrice, Petrarch and his Laura,
Paolo and Francesca, Eloise
And Abelard, Romeo and Juliet—

To these legendary names there clings an aura
Of eternity: yet not just these—
On selfless love the sun will never set.

[111]

PABLO NERUDA'S POPPIES

Poppies—Neruda's nodding butterflies—
Red for blood, white for purity,
Black and purple for widows, mutely defy
Dictators and their sad brutalities.

Yet, whilst they mock man's crude enormities,
What do these fragile emblems signify?
Are they mere bookmarks for the tragedy
Or are they a cover for never-ending obscenities?

Oh, no ... they stand for Hope, and for Remembrance,
For, where these's death, there is rebirth, and renewal—
As Time consumes all, Time can also heal;
Yet Time exacts a purgatorial penance—

How long will be the term of expiation?
What multitudes await an explanation?

from the Spanish of Pablo Neruda

ENVOIE
Three Passages from Jason and Medea, *a version in English of*
The Argonautica *of Appollonius of Rhodes*

I
Hera and Athene Visit Aphrodite

'You alone can smooth the path for Jason':
Thus spoke Hera and paused for a reply.

At first the Cyprian was dumbstruck—
The sight of Hera begging favours filled her
With awe; but when she did regain her tongue
The tone was humble, and conciliatory:
'Revered goddess,' said Aphrodite meekly,
'Consider me the lowest creature living
If I fail you; whatever I can say,
Whatever I can do, whatever strength
These frail hands can offer, are at your service;
Needless to say, I look for no reward.'

Hera responded suavely, and with guile:
'Physical effort is not needed,' said she,
'Hands will not be required; we wish you
Simply to exert a mother's influence.
Persuade your son to cast an amorous spell
And make Aeetes' daughter fall for Jason—
With Medea's help, reclaiming the Golden Fleece
And restoring it to Hellas should be child's play,
For the princess is full of wiles herself'—
Aphrodite now addressed both goddesses:

'My boy has scant respect for me,' she said,
'Though, faced by you, he might display some reverence—
He constantly defies me, nay, revels
In consistently going against my wishes;

I am worn out by his wickedness—indeed,
At times, I have been tempted to break his bow
And cruel arrows right before his face;
He has had the gall to threaten me with them:
'Keep your hands to yourself, Mother,' says he,
'For if I lose my temper you'll be sorry!'

Hera and Athene smiled at her outburst,
Exchanging sidelong glances, but the Cyprian
Was upset: 'You find my woes amusing—
I should keep them to myself, not try to share them—
As for your plan, I will approach Eros—
You have my word, he will not demur'—
Hera held Aphrodite's slender hand,
And, smiling serenely, proffered this advice:
'Do not reproach your boy with too much carping;
He will learn his duty, by and by ...'

II
Eros Takes Wing

Eros carefully counted his knuckle-bones,
Then gave them to his mother for safe keeping.
Snatching his bow, and shouldering his quiver,
He strode through Zeus's orchard, heading for
The Olympian gates; from here, the gods descend
Earthward, but Eros took wing—far beneath,
Twin mountain peaks, earth's tallest, caught the splendour
Of the morning sun—countries, teeming
Cities, sacred rivers, fertile hills;
Populous land, and all-embracing sea ...

Evoë! he comes—passing through the ether,
He lands unseen, intent upon his mischief—
Glancing all around him, stealthily,
He kneels by Jason's feet, and fits the notch

[114]

To the cord; then, drawing at full stretch,
He lets his arrow fly at Medea—
Her heart is pierced, flutters, and stands still—
On carefree wings, Eros swiftly flies
The royal palace, leaving his fatal shaft
Buried within a bosom all on fire.

III
The Flight from Colchis

Jason stood behind her—awestruck, petrified—
But the giant snake, entranced by her sweet voice,
Slowly subsided throughout the entire length
Of his vast, invertebrate body, and lay there mutely
Untangling his innumerable undulations,
Like sea swell settling after an angry storm;
Yet still, the head hovered—gigantic jaws
Gaping—until Medea dipped a sprig
Of juniper in her magic brew; then brushing
His eyes deftly, a deep sleep fell upon him.

The massive jaws closed, and sank to the ground—
The reticulated trunk stretched out behind him,
Measuring the full extent of the sacred precinct—
Medea called out to Jason, who swiftly removed
The Fleece from its protective oak, while she
Was on her knees, smearing the monster's head
With magic ointment; Jason spoke urgently,
Imploring her to leave the gloomy grove
And make for the ship—The Argonaut held
The fabulous Golden Fleece in his arms and rejoiced.

Dawn was shedding its rays across a resplendent
Ocean when they regained the vessel—the crew
Were transfixed when they beheld the Fleece, bright
As a bolt of lightning from the arm of Zeus himself,
Crowding forward to touch and handle it—

But Jason gestured them aside, throwing
A brand new cloak around it for protection,
And escorting the Princess Medea aft to the ship's
Stern, where he made her comfortable. That done,
He turned amidships to address his men:

'Dear comrades,' he began, 'Let us set sail
For home at once. The prize for which we came,
For which we risked our lives on land and sea,
And which cost the lives of many cherished shipmates,
Is ours. The journey has been hazardous;
But now at last, fortune has smiled on us—
Thanks to this brave and noble princess, who,
Herself consenting, I intend to carry home
To Hellas, and there wed—you too, must learn
To love her; our country's deliverer, and our own.'

'I spoke of the need for urgency,
For I feel sure the king and his army
Will challenge us, and that, presently.
If he blocks our passage to the open sea,
All is lost, so man the benches—two
To every seat, taking turns to row—
Those not rowing, hold aloft your shields
As cover against a hail of Colchian arrows.
Children, parents, country, look to us now—
We can plunge them in despair, or grant them glory!'

With that, Jason shouldered arms. The crew
Responded with a mighty cheer, and their leader,
Sword drawn, cut through the hefty hawsers
At the stern. Then, in full battle kit,
He took his place beside Princess Medea
And his trusty helmsman, the worthy Ancaeus.
Argo, that well made galley, leapt sturdily
On strenuous oars towards the beckoning sea,
And every crewman, exerting nerve and muscle,

Pulled mightily to clear her from the river.

The king and all his subjects were apprised
Of what had happened—of Medea's love for Jason,
The crucial part she had played in his success;
Her treason, and her treachery—they were gathered
In full armour in the Agora,
As numberless as waves on choppy seas,
Or swirling Autumn leaves. In his chariot,
Drawn by the wind-swift horses, stood Aeetes,
With round shield, torch, and massive spear;
Holding the reins, his son and heir, Apsyrtes.

The army swarmed along the river banks,
But the stout ship, urged on by the swift current,
And the straining sinews of the stalwart oarsmen,
Was already breasting the first ocean waves;
For Aeetes, it was a bitter pill—enraged,
he raised his arms to Helios and to Zeus,
Calling on them to witness these wicked deeds;
Threatening his own people with extinction
If they failed to bring his daughter back to justice—
Fuming, and raging, in despotic impotence!

That very morning, the Colchians launched their navy;
In desperate haste, but fully fitted out
And ready for a long pursuit—ship's stores
Crammed to bursting with weapons and provisions—
With bright sails flapping, they looked for all the world
Like an army of winged creatures in full cry;
Endless flights of birds, flock on flock,
Assembled as for some mystical migration,
Each chattering squadron in pre-ordained formation,
Breaking the timeless silence of the sea.

Hera whipped up a fresh following breeze

For her brave Argonauts. She was willing Medea
To reach the Pelasgian Land, and quickly too—
There to bring down the House of Pelias—
At daybreak on the third day out, they reached
The coast of Paphlagonia, as predestined.
Medea prepared a sacrifice to Hecate—
What ritual did she follow? My lips are sealed;
But the shrine they raised to the goddess on the shore
Stands inviolate to this very day

***

My tale is told: What hardships and disasters
Yet to befall our brave Argonauts—
How many reached home, how many perished at sea,
Does not concern my story—nor will I say
Whether that bright flame of human passion,
Set ablaze by one divine spark
Ignited by the God of Love himself,
Retained its fire, or turned to dust and ashes.
I leave you with the morning of their love:
Their fate, their future, lies in hands above.

There are varying opinions as to whether notes are either advisable or necessary in a book of verse. I am in favour and for two reasons. I am often allusory and do not presume that readers will share my sometimes recondite interests—an example is 'progressive snooker'—and secondly, I am invariably grateful for any information or reference that sheds light on what I am ingesting. I am hopeful that some of you may share that view.

For the unswerving purist, I offer an uncompromising 'triple haiku' which failed to find a space in the main text and requires no comment— all fifty-one syllables of it!

In my head there is
Nothing to distract me from
This passing moment

If I concentrate
There is no past or future
Just a present tense

Perhaps I have a
Hyperactive temper'ment
I find it boring.

And, may I add, excessively self-centred; but perhaps even that can be a shared experience.

Flight (p. 27)
A simple exercise in definitions, some less familiar than others. For example a flight of locks (on a canal) is a 'close together sequence' as in stairs. The Flight of the Earls of Tyrone, Tyrconnel and Fermanagh took place in 1607.

Inward Eye (p. 28)
Fine-toothed combs, also called Moolie combs were for the removal of unwanted livestock from the scalp and were regularly wielded in primary or public elementary schools in working-class areas for the maintenance of hygiene.

Miching Mallecho (p. 29)
A curious expression used by Hamlet (Act III, Scene 2) which has no satisfactory modern explanation. In Ulster schoolboy parlance, 'miching' or 'mitching' was playing truant.

The Cat's Whisker (p. 30)
An essential element in an early form of wireless called 'A Crystal Set'. My father assembled one in the backyard of our house at 14 Agra Street in order to hear the commentary from America on the heavyweight contest for the championship of the world in 1936.

To Scumble (p. 34)
My recollections of a bit of crack which took place in the old Red Barn pub in Rosemary Street. Scumbling was a technique used by the old-time grainers and marblers in which a transparent glaze of clear varnish was carefully applied at an interim stage of the work.

Pictures in the Fire (p. 35)
'There's a chiel' amang ye takin' names.' A reference to the meeting of Robert Burns and Sir Walter Scott when the latter was only a boy.

Names (p. 36)
Sewage teams clock on as 'green' and 'orange', I learned this bizarre fact from a Channel Four documentary for which I did the original commentary. An executive producer replaced my effort with a female voice. Still, nothing is lost—hence the poem.

Young Pygmalion (p. 38)
An actual happening. As a teenager, one rainy day in the late forties, I accidentally knocked over the famous burlesque star in Bradbury Place Belfast. She was a very gracious lady.

Gospel Truth (p. 41)
Written on a Saturday evening domestic flight from Belfast to London. I was astonished to find the advertisements for churches and gospel halls in the Belfast Telegraph still, in the 1980s upstaging the entertainments pages of London newspapers.

Three Ariel Sonnets (p. 44)
'Sweeney'—Agonisties, Astray and Among the Nightingales are allusions to poems by T.S. Eliot. The Romanian Eugene Ionesco's absurdist play, *The Aerial Pedestrian* prompted the second sonnet, though I must say, that in my dreams, I am myself a fairly regular nocturnal flyer—perhaps I was a bird in a previous existence! Baudelaire's flights of fancy have always intrigued me but the early passionate art criticism is also fascinating and even uplifting!

Domestic Flight (p. 46)
The title poem of the collection. The quotation at its head is from 'Ode to a Tomato' by the Chilean poet Pablo Neruda whose works and memoirs were a focal point of my reading at the time of its composition which took place during a sequence of departures,

from notes made in transit. 'Shadows deep', 'Pilgrim Soul' and 'Moments of glad grace' are echoes of Yeats—the Ronsardian sonnet for Maud Gonne—the opening lines blend in flight service with drowsiness and recollection of the Olivier film of Hamlet and Pathé News. Progressive snooker required only one red to open up a sequence of colours, and this led to bigger breaks. Poppies as butterflies, (Amapolas y mariposas' is a Neruda image from L'Isla Negra; and other imagery includes 'Pablo in wicker chair'—a tableau from his student days in Santiago and Valparaiso. The painter Stanley Spencer's brother Harold played piano in a Belfast dockside bar called Du Barry's. Sailors and old salts who frequented it would likely have been to Valparaiso and Whistler painted a twilight scene of its harbour. John Field, the Irish composer conceived the nocturne before Chopin did and the impressionistic experience from tram or trolleybus windows has its imaginative counterpart in an aeroplane with a distinctly 'fast forward' or 'rewind' effect on take-off and landing. That is why mental pictures from the Albertbridge Road— 'Nabney's windows', 'three brass balls', 'a marble pillared Orange Hall' and so on, are interspersed with 'lantern slides from drowning aviators. Maj jong is an oriental game. Henry Pottinger was made governor of Hong Kong in 1843, not 1842, but it had to rhyme!

Over the Bridge (p. 55)
A sonnet that reflects artistic exile after the break with Ulster theatre caused by the Over the Bridge controversy. Dedicated to Paddy Devlin, because he, more than anyone after I left, perpetuated popular interest in the play. John Keyes has recently edited a new edition of Sam Thompson's plays with a sound introduction.

Blast (p. 56)
The blowing up of the Club Bar as recounted by Tom Gray.

Domestic (p. 57)
A whimsical meditation on a word, not to be taken too seriously.

Supper at Seven (p. 58)
Written for Sir Harry Secombe's programme, *Highway*, it recalls happy childhood days at the seaside and Aunt Jean's holiday bungalow near Stuckland's Glen overlooking Belfast Lough.

Delores of Carrigeenboy (p. 60)
Written for Dolores McDermott, a sweet girl, who was employed at the Bective Hotel in Sligo and who planned an itinerary for me for a most pleasant day out.

Song (p. 62)
A song that marked the end of an affair.

Nous Nous Taisons (p. 65)
This French lyric by Tristan Dérème echoed for me the tristesse that follows a break up or parting.

N'Anga (p. 66)
Means 'spirit medium' in the Shona language. I use it here as a kind of mantra, or form of address, as of one who is held in thrall. 'Trousers rolled' a reference to T.S. Eliot.

Quand Vous Serez Bien Vieille (p. 68)
The parallel with the Yeats poem for Maud Gonne is unavoidable. My translation ends up 'sous la terre' (beneath the sod) to co-incide with Ronsard's original thought; not 'amid a crowd of stars'.

For the Wedding of Julia and Stephen (p. 69)
The eighteen line lyric encapsulates a secondary hidden form like a lover's ring.

Solitude (p. 70)
In Romanian 'Singuratate'. I heard it on a large screen television in a park in central Bucharest with an instant whispered translation form Romanian actor Jon Haiduc. I painfully worked out my version at a later date with the help of a dictionary and grammar book.

Mioritza (p. 72)
I have discussed this Romanian folktale in the introduction and its symbolism no doubt says things to each individual who comes across its deceptively simple message. My concern has been to assemble the basic elements of the tale and deliver them in a personal and perhaps idiosyncratic manner. The device of insisting that the storyteller is relating the plain, the honest, the shocking truth is entirely my own and I hope that the metre I have chosen coveys a sense of relentless inevitability of the tragedy; as predictable as mortality itself.

Shackleton (p. 78)
The name of the home providing sheltered accommodation for the elderly, many of whom were in the advanced stages of Alzheimer's disease. The poem is an impression only of one particular visit, but names have been altered to respect privacy. Bill, however, was my late father-in-law. Shackleton was also the name of a wartime bomber used by the RAF in which he served.

Long Haul (p. 81)
The purple patches seen from the air were both striking and puzzling. They were remarked on by new arrivals other than myself. There is a kind of purgatorial symbolism about airport terminals—the

inevitability on entry and awareness of a point of no return. Arrival, especially with customs formalities, induces claustrophobia. The jacaranda, though not an indigenous tree, is a national symbol in Zimbabwe. It is also ubiquitous.

Tree Studies (p. 89), *On the Wing* (p. 91), *Destinations* (p. 93)
Vegetation, wildlife and placenames are all exotic in Africa, the latter because of the incongruous blend of the tribal and the colonial—the familiar and the foreign. Heightened awareness as well as stunning contrasts speeded up the learning process and I was surprised at how quickly I began to recognise and name quite a wide variety of trees, birds and other wildlife.

The Road to Glenlivet (p. 94)
Actors in faraway places bond and form friendships more readily than when at home. Thanks to Suzanne's insistence that we all acquired wide-brimmed tropical headgear, our intrepid quartet has been named 'The Great Zimbabwe Hat Club' and it is very exclusive. Great Zimbabwe is one of the wonders of Africa but it just outside the scope of the poem—the long day's journey ended at Glenlivet.

Shona Woman (p. 101)
I scribbled this onto a table napkin in a cafe in Harare. The woman, who was very beautiful, was standing at the bar and giving her undivided attention to a man seated on a barstool who was built like an American footballer. It was a spontaneous sketch from the life and required no editing or retouching.

From the Greek (p. 103)
The epigram, or inscription, has an immediacy and spontaneity about it which is sometimes dimmed by the mists of time or by the quaint anonymity of the person or place addressed. To substitute modern Belfast for ancient Athens, or to imagine a memorial to a contemporary rather than an archaic pugilist is fun. Plus ca change! There is nothing new under the sun!

The Bottom Line (p. 104)
This overall title for the sequence of fourteen sonnets is not my own, but it has somehow crept in. 'The bottom line' and all such cliches as 'at the end of the day' and so on, set my teeth on edge. The last named expression particularly infuriates me especially when uttered by an unctious politician in patronising tones, and who, after repeating the empty phrase five or six times in a minute or so, ponderously persists in trying to make it sound meaningful. The sequence, as should be obvious, begins with a mild attack of writer's block. The sonnet which begins 'The man is going abroad ... ' was inspired by yet

another Romanian source. Prince Dimitrie Cantemir of Moldova one of those universal scholars who was both a scientist and a man of letters, a philosopher as well as a ruler, was worried that his subjects were becoming lazy and careless in their everyday speech and that impurities and irregularities were creeping into the language that had been handed down from the time Trajan, particularly in regard to syntax and word order. He took as an example the following sentence. 'The man is going ... to cut ... wood ... for the winter.' Then he inverted it: 'To cut wood for the winter to the forest the man is going.' He made me think.

Pablo Neruda's Poppies (p. 112)
Some years ago now, after a certain South American dictator had gracefully stepped down as head of state, some of the regime's torturers and interogators were interviewed for British television and were seen and heard expressing regret and showing remorse for their actions, in some instances being confronted with their surviving victims, including women who had been sexually abused, and on whom they had inflicted unspeakable agonies. I had been experimenting not very successfully with what for me is a reverse process of translation—rendering English texts into French. After watching the programme, I went out to a restaurant that was being run at the time by an Argentinian friend of mine call Miguel. Armed with a notebook and a Spanish dictionary I decided to try expressing my feelings in a language of which I have only a tourist's grasp. There, sustained by an excellent bottle of Rioja Riserva, and assisted by occasional promptings from my friend who was taking orders, I came up with this poem which has recently acquired a surprisingly contemporary resonance. I am particularly grateful to Miguel for the expression 'Corte de mangas' (cut of the sleeves) which is just a verbal description of a silent, dismissive gesture of contempt, and also for conveying to me all the shades of feeling that are embraced by that lovely Spanish word 'recuerdo'. The English translation of the fourteen lines is a pale shadow of the Spanish, but I seem to remember that Miguel responded favourably to my effort.

Jason & Medea (p. 113)
My title. The Argonautica is the full description of all four books by Appollonius of Rhodes. The whole exercise began with only the lines where Aphrodite complains to the other goddesses about her son's naughty behaviour and my version was mean as a sort of parable or fairytale for the edification of our small son Toto who was only nine at the time and had given his mother a bit of a trying day. The whole piece is of course dedicated to him and he is now a fine big lad of seventeen and doing his A-levels.

The last stanza is not a translation but an addition of my own and may be taken as my signing off lines for the entire book. *Au revoir.*